TECHNOLOGY, TEAMWORK, & EXCELLENCE

BY RUSHTON HURLEY

NCEA.
National Catholic Educational Association

ISBN: 978-1-55833-709-1
Part Number: TEC-70-1610

TABLE of Contents

Foreword V

Introduction VII

STORIES OF EXCELLENCE 1

Chapter 1: Describing Distinctions, Explaining Experiences 3

Chapter 2: Stories of Distinction 7

Chapter 3: Tech and Sharing the Good News of Your School 11

Chapter 4: Funding and Innovation 15

Chapter 5: Tech and Compassion 17

    Conveying Tone 17

    Discussion and Heart 18

    Community and Charity 19

INSPIRING INTERACTION 21

Chapter 6: Tech and Meaningful Learning 23

    Using Examples 25

Chapter 7: Tech and Vibrant Discussion 29

Chapter 8: Tech and Meaningful Feedback 33

Chapter 9: Tech and Major Change 37

    Value of the Change 39

    Transparency of the Process 39

    Progression as Promised 41

BUILDING A TEAM 43

Chapter 10: Tech and Hiring Teachers, Part 1 - Those Who Can Take the Reins 45

Chapter 11: Tech and Hiring Teachers, Part 2 - Teachers and Technology 49

Chapter 12: Tech and Hiring Teachers, Part 3 - Going Deeper 53

Chapter 13: Tech and Hiring Teachers, Part 4 - Interviewing and Being Interviewed 57

FOSTERING EXCELLENCE 59

Chapter 14: Teacher Resilience and Documentation 61

Chapter 15: Identifying and Expanding on Strengths 65

Chapter 16: Valuing the Stories of the Entire Team 69

Chapter 17: The Aspirin Teacher and the Log of Good Moments 73

Chapter 18: Psychology and Excellence 77

Chapter 19: Excellence and the Leadership Team 81

Chapter 20: Modeling Reliability 85

THE FINISH 87

Chapter 21: Fostering Loyalty 89

    Inspiring Experiences 90

    Dedicated Professionals 90

    Regular Storytelling 91

FOREWORD

As a superintendent with a passion for educational technology, I was feeling on top of the world. Our students were learning, the teachers and school administrators were flourishing and we had the very best technologies available.

We had teachers traveling the globe, winning tons of awards, presenting and learning. Of course, this crew did not travel home lightly; they plundered the talents of teachers and technology companies on every journey, returning to pay forward their new teaching trasure to everyone.

On May 3, 2013, I received a piece of this treasure, as our two best technology coaches introduced me to Rushton Hurley.

I had what I thought was a great plan that would designate generous amounts of iPads, PC mobile labs, and Mac mobile labs to particular grades and classes. Excited to finally meet him and pick his brain, I quickly laid it all out. Truthfully, I expected to hear how incredibly supportive, technology-rich, and cutting edge we were. Rushton paused, smiled and responded.

"Cool question. Can you imagine how great it would be if all of your students graduated being device agnostic? Imagine they just grab whatever device makes sense, no matter who makes it."

Imagine? Yeah, I really could. We all could. And a Catholic school superintendent publicly claiming to be agnostic? That led to many future laughs as I presented to others wanting to mirror our successes.

This humbling moment, kindly crafted and offered with a smile from Rushton, put the right devices in the hands of students and teachers. Students responded to the new pedagogies and the division posted even greater learning results at the top of all provincial data charts.

Rushton is much revered and a favored leadership consultant to many Catholic schools throughout North America. In Catholic schools, we are very familiar with parables; often, a rhetorical question does the heavy lifting. Rushton's uncommon sense and fascinating stories force us to think deeply. It is such a rare talent to interrogate reality non-stop, yet leave only a positive wake.

In his newest offering, Rushton is generous with fascinating lessons from around the world where we learn how we can better use technology to grow and celebrate stewardship, build leadership capacity and foster creativity with meaningful learning opportunities.

Technology, Teamwork and Excellence, much like its author, is an impactful, motivating treasure.

Aubrey Patterson
Superintendent (retired)
Lloydminster Catholic School Division
Alberta, Canada

INTRODUCTION

Thank you for picking up this book.

The ideas I share are designed to help Catholic school leaders consider, use, and build upon good practices with tools of technology. Doing this well can make your schools places that are personally and professionally more satisfying for your team, and also more inspiring for your students.

We are well past the time that the presence of computers and other technology by itself somehow conveyed something distinctively positive about a school. When we thought these things before, we were missing the more valuable questions that can make the very important choice of a school something that would frame a child's hopes and decisions for decades to come.

The better questions cover how we use what we have, how we share the stories of our successes, and how we as a team of educators build a culture of exploration for everyone.

If you haven't received questions from prospective parents along these lines, you soon will.

Our rapidly changing world calls for people of faith to assert that honesty, curiosity, and dedication do not simply have a place with what technology makes possible. These traits also allow us to guide the development of new tools and techniques in ways that strengthen our hope for something better.

I pray you find the ideas and stories intriguing, valuable, and inspiring.

Twice in one morning.

The sentence above may generate all sorts of ideas for you. Two championships. Two resignations. Two fits of make-you-cry laughter. Two failures of the network. Two compliments on a member of the staff given by different parents.

Here, this sentence is about how educators think of their schools.

For me, it was one morning in Idaho. Talking with an elementary school principal, I was struck when he said about the school he leads, "This is the first school I've been where I would be completely comfortable having my daughters be in any teacher's classroom."

That's a lot of confidence in one's staff.

Later in the morning, I was reading *Capturing the Spark*[1], by David Cohen, when I encountered this thought again. The book is a set of stories from Cohen's year crisscrossing California to observe great teachers in their classrooms. Early in the book he quotes award-winning middle school teacher Tom Collett talking about the school where he works in the San Francisco Bay Area: "There's so much positive energy...I'd be glad to have my son in any classroom at this school. Any teacher. Roll the dice."

For any teacher or leader, I think this allows a seriously honest look at one's setting. Would you be comfortable having your own child in the care of any teacher on campus? Absolutely any teacher?

My guess is that few teachers would be comfortable with a response of anything along the lines of, "Yes. Roll the dice."

If you are in such a setting, that's wonderful. Whatever your role, make sure you are actively working to keep your very strong team at that level.

If not, then the question that arises is, "Can we get to this point?"

Another way to ask the kind of question that raises the bar in this fashion is, "What will it take for every member of our team to be professional, creative, organized, encouraging, and inspiring?"

My hope for the reader is that the ideas in this book help launch discussions and initiatives that can allow the leaders of any Catholic school to build the kind of team mentioned above.

After all, what's the alternative? Being satisfied with having weak links in the chain? Accepting that the team doesn't work together to build on its strengths? Keeping quiet the stories of success that could inspire the community to support you and your teachers in new ways?

I expect that anyone picking up a book on possibilities for helping a school be something special would find such alternatives unacceptable.

There's always a way to get to where you're going. The ideas in the chapters that follow are designed to help you get there.

The path may be a difficult one, but as was observed by a Chinese philosopher many centuries ago, a journey of a thousand miles begins with a single step.

The walking wild by Hugues de Buyer-Mimeure from Unsplash.

There are steps a team can take with technology that help a school of faith to improve as places of hope and inspiration.

We will take one specific path - looking at the role of technology for bringing out the best in our students, our colleagues, and ourselves - for making schools places that the community can celebrate.

As a frame, know that the complexities will not typically be with the tech, but with the often very personal decisions about how to rise above what makes us comfortable.

I write this book with the hope that my experiences around the world will help you see new possibilities in yourself and your school. I have been blessed to work with leaders and teachers in many different settings, and have seen the magic that results from their work to use what is new to enhance long-developed strengths coming from commitment, faith, and service.

May what you read allow you to inspire and be inspired.

1 *Capturing the Spark* by David Cohen (2016) (available at: https://www.amazon.com/gp/product/0997686804/)

STORIES OF EXCELLENCE

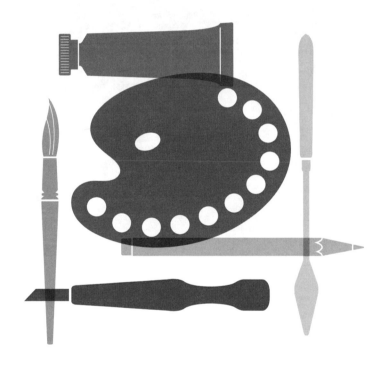

CHAPTER 1

Describing Distinctions, Explaining Experiences

For many, and perhaps most, of the families that consider your school, that their children would get a Catholic education is just the start of a process. It gets parents through the door, but it may well not be enough for a decision to enroll[1].

What prospective families need is to hear what is exceptional and distinctive about your school. This is surely not news to you. Whether you know how to convey both what distinguishes your school, and also a genuine excitement about what their children would do if they enroll, is another matter.

Parents want to hear, and even better, see, what it is that children actually do when in the care of your team.

Start by knowing that a clear description of what students would experience, come home, and describe will trump abstract pedagogical language for almost everyone.

Consider the following:

"Our teachers are well trained in techniques for integrating differentiation within the curriculum to tap the talents of each child in exploring his or her academic development."

And then this:

"The theme in your child's grade level is 'The World Around Us,' and each quarter, every student researches a country to learn about its culture and history. We have connections to schools around the globe, so students also talk with kids their age in those countries using video conferencing tools."

Which sounds more compelling to you?

If you are steeped in educational jargon, you might find the focus of the former more important.

If you are part of the rest of humanity, the latter gives you much more clarity about what choosing your school will give the family the chance to discuss when their children come home each day.

At a time when a child's typical day might be substantially different from what parents experienced at the same age, the need in the family to have regular and positive interaction can't be overstated. Consequently, providing educational experiences that allow parents and children to connect with each other over learning moments is arguably a top-tier piece of how a Catholic school should minister to its families.

> *At a time when a child's typical day might be substantially different from what parents experienced at the same age, the need in the family to have regular and positive interaction can't be overstated.*

Technology can play a significant role in crafting and conveying these experiences for students. Note that tech's possibilities are intriguing when they translate into what children do, as opposed to what the school merely has.

Perhaps teachers at your school regularly have students use digital video tools to tell the stories of their learning. You might explain to parents that while the idea of making a video might be exciting, it is great cover for getting kids to write more effectively and appreciate the value of revision.

It may be that some of your teachers have students chronicle projects using podcasting tools. Being able to mix audio and voice recordings certainly sounds cool to the students, but your teachers might be guiding them in getting and giving feedback so as to appreciate how messages change for different audiences.

There may be a robotics program at your school in which students are mentored by alumni working in the tech field via visits and/or video conferencing. Such a program can convey an interest in helping students begin to understand the ideas of programming and get encouragement for seeing themselves in fields that may have seemed out of reach before.

Your campus ministry program may use digital photography to help students develop empathy for others. You can explain that drawing on powerful images to get students to begin considering the range of concerns and challenges others face is part of your work to help students see beyond themselves.

What matters is not what the school has, but how it is used, and what possibilities this creates for all sorts of students.

It is also important to note that many parents have well-grounded fears about technology.

As just one example, there is the seemingly all-consuming presence of social media in the lives of the young. Today in many schools, bullies use social media to put and keep pressure on their victims. Good schools use the same tools as part of the work to help students know there are people ready to help battle bullying, depression, and other challenges.

These are different times, and so different approaches may be required for timeless problems such as bullying. Families rarely know how to guide their students with tools for which they have less expertise than their children, and strong programs that help both students and families with these challenges can be a major draw[2].

Programs that explain not just the negatives of social media, but also the good use your school makes of these tools may well differentiate your school from others, and parents want to know when they interview you that you and your team are prepared to help and guide them.

As educators in a Catholic school, we can consider the words of Pope Francis: "No family drops down from heaven perfectly formed; families need constantly to grow and mature in the ability to love[3]."

Great schools have students go beyond checking off imposed requirements. They help children learn to explain to others, including their families, how what they learn connects with what they consider important.

As we explore the variety of possibilities for technology, of strategies for building teamwork, and of approaches to fostering excellence, we will return again and again to the core message of schools as being places of inspiration not for what the schools have, but for what the children actually do.

So, what do the students at your school do? Are examples of their work in their own voices available to prospective families?

1 The Catholic School Choice: Understanding the Perspectives of Parents and Opportunities for More Engagement by Foundations and Donors Interested in Catholic Activities and the National Catholic Educational Association from NCEA.org (available at https://www.ncea.org/NCEA/Learn/Resource/Leadership_and_ Governance/National_Perspective/The_Catholic_School_Choice__Understanding_the_Perspectives_of_Parents.aspx)

2 Young People, The Faith And Vocational Discernment, Pre-Synodal Meeting Final Document, 2018 (available at http://www.synod2018.va/content/synod2018/ en/news/final-document-from-the-pre-synodal-meeting.html)

3 Amoris Laetitia, 2016, p255 (available at https://w2.vatican.va/content/dam/francesco/pdf/apost_exhortations/documents/papa-francesco_esortazione-ap_20160319_amoris-laetitia_en.pdf)

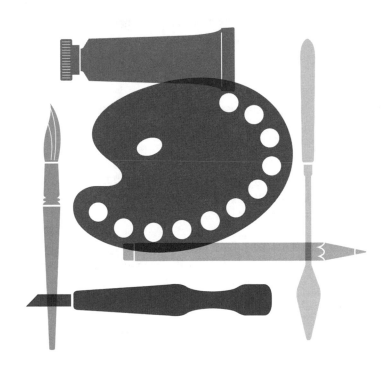

CHAPTER 2

Stories of Distinction

Families probably have more options for schools now than ever before. You probably know what makes your school distinctive, but do families in the community? Does your staff? Are there examples of opportunities for students that everyone on the team knows to point to when asked about the school?

How you work to make sure the team can clearly and concisely articulate the school's strengths will have much to do with how many applicants your school gets. With so many other public and private (both brick-and-mortar and online) schools of choice available, your team's message can determine whether your school thrives or fades.

In my time consulting with schools, I have spent almost three hundred days over the last decade at Junípero Serra High School. Serra is a Catholic high school for boys in San Mateo, California, and I have acted as a technology and instruction coach for its leaders, teachers, and staff.

Dr. Gary Meegan and Dr. Laura Ramey are two theology teachers I worked with for several years before one moved from the area. Together they fashioned a strong social justice project that all students in senior theology would explore as the primary focus of the class.

The project involves researching a chosen cause in detail, conducting interviews, writing and revising descriptions of their work with the cause, reflecting on all aspects of the project in blog posts, and creating a web site exploring the issues involved.

Why are the final two components above powerful for learning?

The blog posts involve reflection, which is an integral component of any truly memorable learning project, and the web site involves carefully crafted written work, which is a focus of every strong school I've encountered.

Neither of these items required technology, and arguably could have been done successfully with chalk and slate.

What the blogs and sites do make possible, though, are two elements that may serve to distinguish any school.

First, there is the reach technology allows. Both blogs and sites can be shared as links easily and without any limitation of distance. Involving supporters of the school generally and the students specifically is far easier when a link can be sent via an email, a text, a social media post or similar.

Second, these forms of expression make it easy to show prospective families what students do at the school. Any high school can be a place where a representative describes what happens, but not all go to the trouble of showing actual academic work to parents curious about the school. Those that show impressive examples of student work are clearly at an advantage over those that don't.

When working to choose a school, parents learn about their options however they can. Test scores, graduation rates, etc., are available online with varying degrees of accuracy. Public-facing programs in athletics and performing arts are easy to research, as well.

What parents want to know, and too often have trouble finding, is what the child will actually do in class.

A particularly impressive example of this is the video created by students at Bishop Sullivan Catholic High School in Virginia Beach, Virginia[1]. For their Senior Evangelization Projects, students made videos about Catholicism. The teacher, John Goerke, wanted to honor the best ones via the inspiration that came to him from Bishop Robert Barron and his work sharing stories of faith and the church through video. As part of this, Goerke wanted Bishop Barron to help him select the best. How would he make this happen?

Goerke and his students worked together to create a video message for Bishop Barron. In it, they talk about what they've read and done, explain what they are asking from Bishop Barron, and ask everyone else to help share the video on social media to capture his attention.

It worked, and the resulting video has been watched on YouTube almost ten thousand times. Bishop Barron ended up seeing the video and agreed to take part within 24 hours of the start of their campaign to get his attention.

The students who made that video are likely to remember that effort for many years to come.

> **What parents want to know is what the child will actually do in class.**

Generally, when students come home from school and parents ask what happened or what they learned that day, what will the students say?

A child's answer could be, "Nothing." Frustrating and almost certainly inaccurate, that.

Still, hope springs eternal that the child would readily open up with intriguing stories of what everyone learned. Clarity about what happens in class via examples of actual (and easily-shared) learning could be that which tips a family into submitting an application.

If you are a parent for whom strong academic work and a focus on service to others is important, you might well appreciate seeing the kind of work that senior theology students at Serra engage in every year, or the video made by the students at the school in Virginia.

What is it that helps prospective families in your area understand your school's strengths? How easily shared are the examples and stories?

1 "Theology Teacher Goes Viral with Digital Evangelization Project" from Bishop Sullivan Catholic High School Homepage News (available at https://www.chsvb.org/news-detail?pk=947911) (video available on YouTube at https://www.youtube.com/watch?v=3lZ3mhYJ_OE)

CHAPTER 3

Tech and Sharing the Good News of Your School

In some communities, the stories you hear about a school are partially correct, but the correct parts apply to the situation at the school two or three decades before.

One elementary school I have worked with is a place where teachers work together energetically to create possibilities for their students. There's an impressive and welcoming area where families in need can get food and clothing. Students make videos about great projects happening at every grade level.

Others in the area may only know about the poverty in that part of the city. They may be aware that serious dysfunction once existed on the staff.

In many schools like this, people in the community bemoan the school's problems, oblivious to how those problems are being addressed, or even that some problems were handled successfully. They also are utterly unaware of the current challenges. For so many schools, the current challenges are ones these same people could easily help address, if they weren't mired in conversations about long-dead issues.

Where does fault lie for such a sorry situation?

The gossips? No.

Fault lies at the feet of the leaders of the school.

It is not the responsibility of the community to understand and promote a school's accomplishments and efforts. The community's job is to work with the information available about what happens at the school. For too many schools, the leadership hasn't provided the community with meaningful information to help them understand both the strengths and the challenges the school faces.

It may be that there are many good stories about the school's strengths, but there hasn't been a way to regularly find and celebrate them.

There could be information about the school shared in an associated church, but it's on a board that few see, and isn't normally discussed when the church community is together.

It may be that information is provided, but in only one direction, and members of the community haven't had a chance to engage with leaders, asking what they can do to help.

It may be that the challenges have been kept quiet, and the hints of what might be a problem have become inaccurate stories, and are now creating new challenges.

Clearly privacy concerns mean being careful about some issues. However, if the school's leadership constantly errs on the side of not providing enough information, opportunities to tap the community's talents and ideas for addressing challenges may be lost.

It also may be that there are plenty of stories the school shares with the community, but there may be a disconnect between what people hear and what leaders meant to convey.

All of the above is to say that, as in the classroom, the difference between broadcast and reception is key.

A teacher who puts material in front of the students, but not in a way that allows them to learn, cannot in good conscience complain about students' poor performance. That teacher's job is to do everything possible to figure out what his or her students need. Not every student will respond, but if the teacher hasn't bothered to seek different ways to get a message across, it's hard to blame the unlucky students who were assigned to that classroom.

Similarly, if a school leader chooses only one or two methods of sharing successes (newsletter, Facebook, etc.), and does nothing else, it's hard to blame people in the community, many and perhaps most of whom need other avenues for discovering and celebrating what students are doing.

> *Strong communication requires understanding the difference between broadcast and reception.*

Typically, one of the problems of conveying these stories is gathering them.

Every school, it seems, asks for teachers to share what happens in classrooms. In essence, this is a directive to evangelize for the school. Many teachers hold back, however, because they feel that they're bragging when telling about the good things that happen in their classes. They feel this way because they are humble, or because they are concerned that colleagues will react poorly to their sharing successes, or both. It's also possible they simply don't see the good they do as something that is distinctive and should be shared.

Getting teachers at any school to understand their important role in gathering the content that the school uses for promotion is no small challenge. Much like a teacher explaining something only one way, the leader should be clever about ways to tease stories from the larger team.

Another school I've worked with has a novel approach for making this happen.

I have been blessed to visit some amazing schools all over the world. Among the best is a private PK-12 school in Cape Town, South Africa, called Parklands College.

It is impressive for many reasons, and among them is how they have acted to help teachers become comfortable sharing the stories of the learning that happens on their campus.

Each summer, all teachers take a photography class to help them learn about such things as composition, angles, and lighting. The idea, of course, is that when they have students doing activities, teachers have a much better sense of what kind of shots might yield good visual material for those handling PR for the school

The class does more than just generate good images, though. Having the shared experience of learning something together creates conditions for teachers to more effectively discuss how they convey stories of learning.

It also allows them to have points of connection that go beyond day-to-day concerns. In many schools, the team's conversations rarely venture into the kind of exploratory territory that can make an educator's work reach another level of fascinatingly meaningful, and an important question for any school leader centers on what brings out exploratory conversations among the team.

For any given group, there is something that can move people past what merely keeps things running, and for many settings, an inspirational story is the first thing to try.

An American college called Strayer University is one of the best schools I know for taking this approach to opening a conversation about possibilities. They have a team of videographers who work to create short stories which inspire people to imagine their futures in powerful ways.

"What's Your Biggest Regret?" is one of these videos from Strayer[1]. It is a well-crafted piece in which a blackboard is placed next to a sidewalk in New York City. People passing by are invited to take the available chalk and write down their regrets.

The messages mostly cover things not done, such as "not pursuing my passions," "staying in my comfort zone," "not pursuing my MBA," and "not saying 'I love you.'"

A video like this can allow us to ask what we as educators might later regret not doing: "not contacting a student's parents to try to work together," "not giving a child the opportunity to show progress in some other way," "not sharing what I saw on the playground," or "not telling my students I am proud to be their teacher."

Compelling stories can get us past the barriers of cynicism and frustration that often keep us from stretching ourselves in the hope we can accomplish more than we have before.

A short video with an inspirational and/or intriguing story can be used to get people generating ideas. These videos are collected in many places, and over the years I have put dozens into the resources section of NextVista.org[2].

> ## *Barriers of cynicism and frustration often keep teachers from stretching themselves.*

At core, the more we try, the more successes we generate.

The more successes we have, the more they can become compelling stories for our community.

Compelling stories do not just inspire teachers to take the next step to generate an exploratory culture. They also can inspire the community to pay closer attention to a school's strengths, share in its hopes for the students, and support the school's efforts in new and powerful ways.

How can you help teachers and staff share more of the successes they see, and how will you get these stories into the community?

1 "What's Your Biggest Regret" by A Plus/Strayer University: (available on YouTube at https://www.youtube.com/watch?v=R45HcYA8uRA)

2 "Stories of Inspiration" on NextVista.org: (available at http://www.nextvista.org/resources/inspiration/)

CHAPTER 4

Funding and Innovation

Can students' ideas improve the school? If so, how do they know?

Consider this from an April 2018 post to EdSurge[1]:

> *"During a classroom unit on persuasiveness, the students had to come up with an idea that would help improve their classroom. The proposals—from Yogibos bean bag chairs to a fully-equipped activity room—were presented in front of their classes, school administration and members of the Chappaqua School Foundation, an organization that fulfills grant requests. The innovative solutions were then voted on by students to become fully funded."*

Students often see what they do at school from a painfully passive perspective. Someone tells them what to do, to write, or to remember, and their job is to follow orders.

It is certainly the case that the ability to follow directions is a key skill for taking advantage of any number of opportunities one might encounter. That said, if what seems to be celebrated more than anything else in school is mere compliance, students won't be motivated to come up with the creative ideas that can make for the best moments in our work.

Asking students to brainstorm and pitch ideas for ways to improve the school is an excellent way to let them know their ideas are valued. These ideas may have to do with academics, ministry, promotion, or anything else that they care about.

That others are considering the students' proposals, and might even fund what they suggest, takes things to a much more compelling level for the students.

Leaders at schools where few funds are available might feel that they are unable to provide an opportunity like this to their students, but consider how inexpensively this could be done.

A teacher could tell a class of elementary students that he is going to donate $5 to a cause, but groups in the class will need to work together to make a presentation with a suggestion to determine which cause it will be. Students would have to identify a cause, describe what the money could do to help, and explain why they feel this is important. The process of working through ideas together would make for an interesting learning opportunity all by itself.

> *If what seems to be celebrated more than anything else in school is mere compliance, students won't be motivated to come up with the creative ideas that can make for the best moments in our work.*

One important piece of the EdSurge post is the expansion of the audience for the students' work. You can imagine the value of having members of the group hearing the proposals (in this case, people associated with Chappaqua School Foundation), and sharing the stories of their experience with others. One or more exceptional presentations could become the kind of story that brings more attention, support, and opportunities to your school.

Conveying these stories well will require some preparation. You certainly wouldn't want to get to the end of a great student presentation and think, "I wish we had recorded that."

Rather than suffer such a moment, someone should record the students making their pitches, and this should be part of the practice for the actual presentation to the group that will make decisions. The visuals may be the students facing the camera, or slides that they narrate using a screencasting tool. The former approach can provide visual evidence of students at their best. The latter represents one way of following a school's privacy guidelines.

The recording could be used to help students learn to give and receive feedback, helping them get into the habit of looking for ways they can improve what they have done. A simple web survey would allow them to get feedback from people anywhere in the world who see the recording. In terms of protecting students' privacy, the video can be shared as "private" on YouTube or similar sites.

Funding pitches or another great activity that push students to present an idea well may allow them to see themselves as people whose ideas are valued for improving their school and community. Such presentations might help them see what is possible when they take their effort to another level. An activity like this might be the gift that makes them know they and their ideas matter to others.

Recall the $5 donation promised by the teacher in the example earlier. That $5 could yield a powerful moment of learning, and is probably less than what the teacher spent to decorate some piece of the classroom wall.

Is there a teacher at your school who might give this a try? What can you try and learn together as part of the effort?

---

1 "How a Shark Tank Competition Lets Students Create Their Dream Classrooms" by Hannah Fenlon and Henry Asa on EdSurge.com, posted Apr 19, 2018, and accessed Aug 25, 2018 (available at https://www.edsurge.com/news/2018-04-19-how-a-shark-tank-competition-lets-students-create-their-dream-classrooms)

CHAPTER 5

Tech and Compassion

Just as students know when a teacher cares about them, teachers know when leaders care about their personal and professional growth.

Many highly effective leaders are able to mix compassion and creativity to engender confidence in and create possibilities for those they lead, and technology has a role to play in building the relationships that make a school strong.

How might you use technology to strengthen your ability to be a compassionate leader? Here are several ideas to try.

CONVEYING TONE

As a school leader, how do you encourage teachers who have asked for help to become more effective?

One way is to send messages using digital media tools rather than email.

Any message of encouragement, whether written or spoken, is most effective when you have taken time to get your wording just right. The relationship will dictate the nature of the message, but sometimes what proves most effective for those you mentor is as much a function of your tone as of your words.

Use your voice both to strengthen the message for the teacher you are helping, and also to let yourself reflect on how you control tone in your own communication.

Simple tools, such as voice recorders or the camera on a smartphone, can allow you to hear and tweak how you sound when conveying a message.

SpeakPipe Voice Recorder, for example, allows one to record oneself using any device, creating a link to share with others[1]. Use this tool or anything like it to record a message of encouragement for one of your teachers, and then listen to how it sounds. Does your voice convey how you feel? Will the teacher hear both the message and your tone? Is there anything in either message or tone that will distract from what you want to convey?

> *Sometimes what proves most effective for those you mentor is as much a function of your tone as of your words.*

DISCUSSION AND HEART

Over the past few years I have presented to many school leaders in small sessions on how to improve staff and team meetings. Conference sessions I run on the topic frequently draw good crowds, and it's always interesting to me that a shared pain point and a hope for something better would compel conference attendees to spend time in a session on staff meetings.

In it, we explore using survey tools to gather the positives on a campus and provide leaders the chance to highlight the work and observations of people across the staff. We also discuss building what I call an "exploratory culture" to strengthen teachers' ability to brainstorm together.

Another element of the training covers how to build a positive tone by using a powerful story to prepare the team for a discussion.

As background, I believe that we frequently know in our heads what needs to happen at a school, but may not have the push from our hearts to act on what we know.

A well-crafted, short video can address that disconnect powerfully.

The example I show in these sessions is a story about a man named Mick Ebeling, who decides to act after reading about a South Sudanese boy who lost his arms in a landmine explosion[2]. Ebeling travels to Africa, and works with the villagers to set up a computer and 3D printer so that they can create prosthetic arms and hands. It's an impressively crafted video, and powerfully moving.

At one point, Ebeling says, "I have a process. And the process is, you commit, and then you figure out how the heck you're going to do it."

In asking for impressions after showing the video, invariably someone mentions this line. It gives us the chance to talk about discussions centered on what we can try, vs. what keeps us from being able to accomplish something.

You likely have children who regularly generate challenges at your school. Do you believe that finding a way to reach those children and help them get excited about their possibilities is important?

If you take seriously what it means to be an educator, the answer is, "Yes."

That means working with a group to make a priority out of figuring out what hasn't been tried, what hasn't been tried well, and what the next steps are to pursue.

There is little better in our professional lives than helping a challenged child accept what learning can offer. Promoting conversations on your staff using stories that keep the focus on this is one way to let compassion drive your work.

Your next meeting might be the perfect setting to try it.

COMMUNITY AND CHARITY

Those of us working in Catholic schools know well the importance of fostering a sense of service in our students, and many schools require completing some amount of service to the community by volunteering in eligible charities.

This stewardship of our talents and resources might be something small scale within the parish, or it might be time devoted in conjunction with many thousands of others as part of global efforts to help those in need.

When engaged in service activities, what do we ask of our students? A signed page showing the number of hours the student spent as a volunteer? A written reflection on what the experience meant to them?

While there is nothing intrinsically wrong with either, a lack of audience for conveying what one has done can make the service requirement more of a box to check off than a meaningful personal experience.

Several years ago at Junípero Serra High School in San Mateo, California, students in Ed Taylor's freshmen theology class created short videos about local charities. The students researched charities to get to know their stories, spent time engaged in service activities, and interviewed volunteers. They put together short videos and shared them with the charities, then submitted the videos to a contest to try and earn the charities an extra donation[3].

In this work, students went well beyond their usual requirements for service hours. They finished with stories that could help the charities share their mission and gather new support and volunteers. Along the way, students discovered that their digital media skills could be of immediate value to others in the community.

> *A lack of audience for conveying what one has done can make a service requirement more of a box to check off than a meaningful personal experience.*

This can prove to be a compelling way to help prospective families see what happens at the school, as well.

How can you help your school's community use voice, story, and video to foster compassion and excellence?

1 SpeakPipe's free voice recording tool allows for recording up to five minutes, and the link to what is recorded will stay active for three months (as of the time of writing). Following the link also will display a download option to get the file as an MP3. Make sure to go directly to the voice recorder link (available at http://speakpipe.com/voice-recorder), as the main page will confuse one looking for just the voice recorder.

2 Find the Mick Ebeling "Look Inside" by Intel and Mick Ebeling on YouTube (available at: https://www.youtube.com/watch?v=ol19tt3VWhQ)

3 Learn more about Next Vista for Learning's Service via Video contest at the contest page (http://nextvista.org/projects/serviceviavideo/). Find the set of contest winners, including several from JSHS, in the NextVista.org service videos library (http://www.nextvista.org/tag/projectwinner/).

INSPIRING INTERACTION

CHAPTER 6

Tech and Meaningful Learning

How do students know that their own work is good?

Some years ago, I visited an impressive middle school in Monterrey, Mexico. Students in one class were working on a digital book, complete with researched passages they had written by the text group, interactive games by the programming group, and videos made by the digital media group.

Knowing of my work with educational videos, my host introduced me to the digital media group, and the students asked if I would like to see their work. I let him know I was happy to see what they had done.

> After the first short video finished, they looked at me with smiles on their faces, awaiting my reaction.
>
> "This is good," I said.
>
> They beamed.
>
> I then added this question: "How do you know it will help someone?"
>
> An awkward pause ensued.
>
> "What do you mean?" asked one of the students.
>
> "Well, you've made a video that's supposed to teach students something. How do you know it will do that?"

Quickly, their expressions became more interested, and a strong conversation kicked into gear.

After talking with them a bit more, I summed up my thoughts.

"I really think this is good, but I also think you should be able to explain why."

I could see in their faces that this was a group of kids who would quickly learn to answer that question.

When pointed out that they could take their work a step further, they might have bemoaned that they were being asked to do anything more than they had already done. I have certainly run across many children and adults like that. At this school, though, there is a culture of rising to challenges, and the kids themselves find such challenges interesting.

Strong school leaders are people who help people regularly rise to challenges on their campuses. They understand that technology is a vehicle for exploring new challenges, for making those challenges compelling to the students, and for making the most of opportunities to celebrate students' pushing themselves to another level.

Video certainly is not the only way to test this in a classroom, but it's a good way for capturing the creative imagination of many students.

In exploring this, you might ask if a teacher is willing to allow students, at least once in a while, to show their mastery of content and connections to other learning with something like video. Plenty of teachers who do not know how to make a video would cut off the opportunity for the students, simply because they (the teachers) haven't learned the tools and processes the students would use.

One might hear, "How can I ask them to do something I can't teach them?"

One response, "Do you really expect them to limit themselves only to what you know?"

When students have choices, it opens the door to the teacher being surprised by what a student might bring to an assignment, and these surprises can be the most memorable moments in teaching.

Once a teacher is willing to let students do something like create a video, the question changes: will the teacher help students hold themselves to a high academic standard?

Too many student video projects are blessed as finished by the teacher simply because a video has a start and an end. Regardless of subject, though, the teacher's job isn't to note the completion of the video, but to check whether students have shown mastery, insights, and connections in their learning.

That is, don't be satisfied with getting in the car. Make sure you actually drive it where you want to go.

> *Do your teachers expect students to limit themselves*
> *only to what the teachers know?*

Video done well can incorporate more than just a well-crafted story. Getting a video from idea to compelling product also involves students learning to become comfortable with feedback. That process can look something like this:

1. Get at least four other students to provide thoughts on your project that are meaningful—"good," "cool," and the like don't rise to the measure of "meaningful".

2. Thank each person for the feedback provided. Do not debate the merits of the feedback at the moment you get it, though you can ask clarifying questions.

3. Keep a feedback log of what was suggested and by whom, whether you choose to incorporate the suggestion, and why you chose what you did in detail.

4. Turn in both the draft and the revision, along with the feedback log.

If videos are kept short (i.e., focused on the learning, with no lame blooper reel at the end) and the students have brought creative insights to what they put together, the result can be useful well beyond the class for which it was made.

Campus and team leaders may incorporate such videos into PD efforts, using them to discuss what distinguishes in this medium strong academic work from weak.

They may use it for PR purposes, showing it at a back-to-school event, or posting it to the school's social media accounts.

USING EXAMPLES

Another component of meaningful learning is the ability to know where the strengths and weaknesses are in one's work. Technology can play an important role in helping students look past simply completing something and thinking about what elements of their work can be exceptional.

Take a class presentation assignment using a slides tool such as Google Slides, Apple Keynote, or Microsoft PowerPoint.

We've all seen bad ones, with material copied from heaven knows where, images (or clip art!) with a tenuous connection to the content, and presenters reading their slides with their back to the audience.

Such a memory may make you shudder, but the twitch hopefully will go away.

The staggering volume of bad presentations, however, may have as much to do with the assignment as ignorance regarding quality choices for content and visuals.

Consider how often students are asked to create presentations without having ever been through a meaningful process of evaluating a range of existing ones. Exactly how often that is, I suspect no research is out there to reveal definitively. If my experience is reflective, however, for every one teacher I've encountered who has students do constructive activities of finding and evaluating the presentations of others, there are a hundred who do not.

A single search, using the right code, can provide loads of presentation files that can be used as fodder for discussing what is surprising, offensive, impressive, boring, or intriguing. Here's one type of search for a cell division presentation in Google:

cell division filetype:ppt

Specifically, a search on the above (using exactly the same spacing) would only return PPT files. While PowerPoint certainly isn't a new presentation technology, it is the most widely used over the last two or three decades, and therefore there is more presentation content available online in the PPT format than any other.

What matters is not that it is the latest and greatest technology, but that one can end up with a wide variety of examples for using a presentation tool to convey a message.

Looking at the address in the search result (when using Google, the part in green under the title), use elements of the address ("k12" or "school" or "edu" or similar) to try and guess before looking at the file what the level of the content might be.

From there, students can be asked to examine several presentations they find to determine strengths and weaknesses. Are some more interesting than others, and if so, why? Do some presentations include citations for the information and media in them? If so, can you verify that the citations point to something real?

Once students have the chance to see a variety of approaches to crafting presentations, they will better be able to choose which approaches they should use with their own work.

For many secondary students, this technique of finding presentations online is not new, though how they use the technique may be less than honorable.

They may have used the code above to find material, make a few changes, and turn it in as their own. They save themselves time, but risk getting caught plagiarizing. When they do not understand and appreciate the damage that does to how their teachers perceive them, they may feel the risk is worth the saved time.

Another reason they may choose a dishonorable path, though, is because they simply don't know how to create something that seems any good. That's natural, if they haven't had the chance to look at a variety of examples and learned to consider and discuss strengths and weaknesses.

I should note for teachers that finding plagiarized PowerPoint presentations usually isn't that hard. Use the title or a distinctive phrase in the slides, search on that with the "filetype:ppt" code, and check the first few search results. One rarely need go further, as plagiarists are by definition lazy.

Sample videos and presentations are just two examples of what can become prompts for examining work quality, improving assignments, discussing how different audiences encounter different messages, and sharing what happens at a school.

As a leader, if you haven't used students' work to show the complexity they learn to explore in your school's classrooms, you may need to spend time in some honest reflection as to why.

What student work would you show to demonstrate that meaningful learning happens in your school? Why would you choose that, and for what audience would it be most effective?

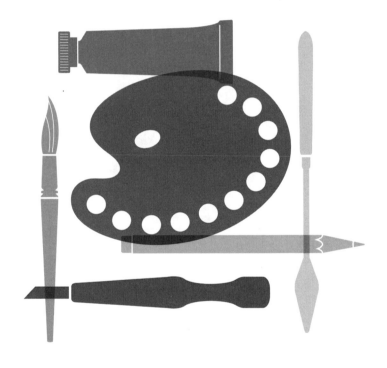

CHAPTER 7

Tech and Vibrant Discussion

Another training I do at many conferences is one focused on using the first minutes of a class or a learning period as productively (and compellingly) as possible.

I ask the teachers to think of anything fascinating they've learned in the last six months or so, and then have them talk with a person or two nearby about what came to mind. Typically, this generates immediate conversation, with people sharing all sorts of ideas.

After a few moments, I ask them to tell what they came up with in an online chat forum of some kind I've created, and then have people look at the other answers in the chat.

I'll then stop the group, and ask for anyone to tell the room what he or she came up with.

Much more often than not, this elicits stares. I'll wait just long enough for this to be a bit awkward, and then grin and make my point.

"Some of you have guessed what I just did. I asked you to talk with each other, and conversations erupted. I asked you to add your thoughts to the chat, and lots of cool things showed up. I asked you to speak in front of the room, and we got silence."

They'll smile, as any who didn't get it before immediately understand my point. Students and teachers both have ideas when prompted, but may not feel comfortable sharing them in front of a larger group. They may share a profession, a commitment to children, and a faith, but that may not mean they will share an idea when you ask.

If confidence sharing ideas is the key to making a classroom a comfortable place for a student to say what they think, it's a fair guess that many teachers feel similarly in staff meetings. I have known many teachers who can speak easily in front of large groups of students, but tend to hold back from sharing thoughts when the group is made up of colleagues.

Seeing such tendencies on your team raises the question of how comfortable people are sharing their thoughts in your staff meetings. This may sound like it's a question about rapport and familiarity, but as above, it's also about the prompt and the vehicle for responding.

What and how leaders ask does much to set the professional tone for the group.

In discussing how to use time well in staff meetings with school leaders, I often recommend starting with a simple survey asking each member of the meeting to share one really cool thing they have seen or heard since the last meeting.

The idea is that over time, people get used to the idea of looking for positives to give when surveyed. It could be a great insight shared in class by a student who doesn't normally contribute. It could be that some students were helpful cleaning up tables in the cafeteria after lunch one day.

Whether big (state championship!) or small (a word of encouragement from one student to another), the idea is that this becomes a topic of exploration—along with a repository of good material for accreditation visits and PR.

The next phase of the meeting may involve the leader taking a few of the answers from the survey from the last meeting, and using those as shout-outs.

Both of the above mean using time with the intention of building positives. Too often, time is used in ways that make teachers feel like the meeting leader is simply checking off boxes (announcements that include detail that could have been in an email, for example).

It's important to know that every decision leaders make about time sends a message about their perceptions of the professionalism of the team. A simple survey using Google Forms or anything like it can both set a good tone, and also gather a variety of items to reach for when something positive is needed.

With a more positive tone, the nature of discussions in staff and team meetings can change, as well.

> *Every decision leaders make about time sends a message.*

Having set a positive tone using a survey and some shout-outs, the meeting can move on to small groups discussing specific stories or possibilities. One might use an inspirational video, a tech tool, or even an image to give the team the chance to make and share creative connections that could be good for the school.

Are your teachers comfortable offering ideas and building off the ideas of others? If not, consider how you ask them for their ideas, as well as what you are doing to set a tone when preparing to have people share their thoughts.

Great schools are places where all people (leaders, teachers, staff of all kinds, students, and supportive members of the community) know they have a voice in exploring possibilities, and build from each discussion toward something worth trying. When and what were the last really strong discussions you had with other members of the school community? Those moments and ideas may help you choose how to spend time with your people, and therefore send important messages about the value of their contributions.

What's an example of a truly powerful discussion on your campus? What came of it? How might you foster more?

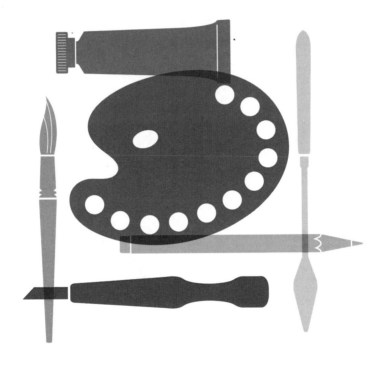

CHAPTER 8

Tech and Meaningful Feedback

Have you ever left a meeting feeling nothing was accomplished? Even when you think the time was well spent, would everyone at the meeting agree that something substantive came from it?

Every choice you make about time sends a message, and you want all your messages to be ones that strengthen a sense of confidence in the team in general, and your leadership in particular.

Some leaders feel that by holding regular meetings (weekly meetings of exactly fifty-five minutes, for example), the group has the opportunity to be reminded who is running things and that reporting on activities to that person's satisfaction is each member's responsibility.

The message you broadcast, however, may be somewhat different than the one the team receives.

They may see the meetings as evidence that the leader is more interested in constant recognition of his or her status than in showing confidence in the talents of the team or even focusing on challenges the school faces.

I should note that I am not against regular meetings, nor do I have any problem with a period of fifty-five minutes. Making sure that meetings conform to regularity of occurrence and length, though, could be doing more harm than good.

At core, what most want from a meeting is no mystery:

1. The meeting lasts only as long as needed.

2. It is clear to all participants what is accomplished and what each person should do next.

How can you know participants walk away believing the above, though?

First, they must trust that they can be honest with you. Any professional culture in which this is in doubt has much deeper problems than the content of any given meeting. Leaders who are seen as manipulative, deceptive, or simply into their own authority in even small ways undercut their own ability to gather accurate information and act in a way that the school needs.

Leaders who listen carefully, explain their choices, and value the input of others, are in a position to earn the trust of everyone.

With meetings, leaders can strengthen the team by providing the opportunity for attendees to share their impressions. Finishing with a simple three-item survey can facilitate this:

1. Was the length of the meeting too short, too long, or just right?

2. What do you feel we accomplished?

3. What are your action items going forward?

There are many tools for creating simple surveys for questions like those above. As so many schools now use Google's offerings for education, a simple survey made in Drive using Google Forms is a good approach. Because the answers feed a spreadsheet that is easily accessed and shared, the team can work together to track whether action items are handled effectively.

In addition to individual surveys, it is typically a good idea to ask for other comments or thoughts, as well. This gives team members the chance to learn from each other's impressions.

Within meetings, the leader also can develop a sense of the communication patterns of different people in order to better know where misunderstandings within the group are likely to occur. This gives the leader a sense of how each member of the team is best approached with ideas.

Some, for example, are more into statements.

"We should do such and such," may be an aggressive challenge to any who think differently. It also may come from someone perfectly willing to be convinced of a different approach, but wants to squarely debate the merits of possible approaches.

Others lead with questions.

"Would such and such be a good move for us?" may be an honest question about strengths and weaknesses of a given course of action. It also may be a polite question coming from one who is only interested in that choice, and who will fume for months if a different path is taken.

The two possibilities described above are a good starting point for a leader's work to understand how to approach members of a team. Working with the communication pattern a person normally uses won't guarantee keeping that person happy, but may optimize the chances that interactions stay constructive.

When asking for feedback, subtle differences in questions can go a long way in making sure a conversation doesn't move in an unhealthy direction.

Consider the question of the number of teachers who should be on duty before school each day. "Do you think we have enough teachers on duty before school?" is one way of asking. "What do you think we can do to have drop-off go more smoothly before school?" is another. They may get you to the same place, but based on the personality of the person asked, one may be more constructive than the other.

> **When asking for feedback, subtle differences in questions can go a long way in making sure a conversation doesn't move in an unhealthy direction.**

Some leaders might see adjusting to a different personality to be the responsibility of the team members. These leaders may feel that the members' jobs are to recognize the authority and personality of the leader and communicate in a way that works specifically for the leader.

A skim of even one of the Gospels would quickly convey to a Catholic school leader who thinks this way that he or she is out of alignment with Jesus' example.

In the 10th chapter of Mark, a rich man asked Jesus what one must do to inherit eternal life.

> *Jesus, looking at him, loved him and said to him, "You are lacking in one thing. Go, sell what you have, and give to [the] poor and you will have treasure in heaven; then come, follow me[1]."*

The passage is an interesting one for many reasons, but one element stands out for our discussion: His compassion for the man is mentioned before Jesus explains what he should do. Perhaps He knew that it was both what the man needed to do, but also that he would not bring himself to do it.

Jesus' many interactions with Peter also show that both compassion and teaching continually intertwined to shape the delivery of His messages. The focus was always on who Peter could become; even when Jesus spoke of Himself, it was framed for Peter to help him become the one who would lead the disciples and the church.

Arguably, the job of the school leader is to inspire all members of the school to give their best always. If so, then finding ways to adapt to others' communication patterns in meetings and individually may not just prove helpful for getting constructive feedback; it also may be that which sends an honest message that a leader is humble enough to listen, and intelligent enough to act on what makes the most sense instead of only on what he or she wants.

By using a simple system such as an online survey, a leader can gather, regularly review, and act on feedback. Along the way such leaders become more aware of how team members choose to communicate, and that opens the door to learning how to inspire them.

How do leaders you admire gather and use feedback?

1 United States Conference of Catholic Bishops online Bible (available at: http://www.usccb.org/bible/mark/10)

CHAPTER 9

Tech and Major Change

Major changes at a school offer a dual opportunity: one can build upon an exploratory culture to strengthen teamwork and morale, and one can model the use of technology for collaboration as the change is explored and perhaps implemented.

When done poorly, moving toward a major change can reinforce the belief of some staff that leadership doesn't listen to the team when a new direction is considered. This can easily happen when change is *imposed* rather than *proposed*. How leaders choose to explore and implement changes will send important messages that last beyond the initiative of the moment.

I was able to see an effective exploration of major changes firsthand at Junípero Serra High School, where in the fall of 2013, all students began bringing an internet-connected device to classes, everyone began using Google Apps (now called G-Suite) for the enhanced level of collaboration it allows, and they switched from a period schedule that had been in place for decades to a block schedule.

No small set of changes, those. That they did it all at once might cause an observer to assume some level of insanity on the part of the school's leaders.

As it turns out, though, the surveys at the end of the fall and spring semesters showed that the changes were going very well. Each of the three major changes was considered in the surveys, and the results were 75%-95% supportive with the staff, with even higher positive responses from the students. Because of these strongly affirmative results, they continued the changes into the next year.

I believe that Serra's success was largely a function of all their school and teacher leaders did to communicate their ideas and rationale. Perhaps more impressive still was that they made shifts along the way as teachers identified weaknesses in their plans.

For us, the role of technology in the exploration of change will center on communication, and as an example, we can imagine typical challenges inherent in one of the three elements of Serra's 2013 shifts, and one of the more common major changes over the last decade: the one dealing with students carrying devices to class.

Starting in the mid to late 00's, many American schools begin making a switch to what is called "one to one," a move typically represented as "1:1" in edtech writing.

The numbers refer to internet connected devices and students, with the idea that at any moment in learning, a teacher can ask each student in a class to use a laptop, tablet, or other device to accomplish some task.

Having such tools generates challenges, of course, but also many opportunities: students might discuss bias in information presented online, interpret images from the streets of cities across the planet using maps tools, collaborate on slides designed to introduce their community to students at a partner school in another country, find government data related to pollution in their community, listen to and discuss a children's song from decades ago, draw connections and identify contrasts between different photographs capturing similar moments, etc.

Being able to engage in such dynamic learning activities, however, runs up against the reality that many teachers have never been trained how to have students use these devices effectively in class.

Anyone who has taken part in a move to 1:1 has likely heard these questions:

- "Won't the students become distracted?"

- "What do I do when something inappropriate appears on a student's screen?"

- "What if they ask me how to use a tool that I'm not familiar with?"

This just starts the list of good questions for which the answers may not be obvious to the teachers or the school's leaders.

Teachers in a 1:1 environment are essentially being asked to do things quite differently than they have done before, perhaps for decades. That's a substantial challenge, and so there had better be a good reason for making the move.

Let's look at a question and an answer, as well as focus on how change can be productively explored through trust.

The question: Do most people have trouble shifting from what they have been comfortable doing?

The answer: Do bears defecate in the woods?

The focus: Accepting a shift, and especially a major shift in how one works, requires trust in three pieces of the change process:

1. the value of the change for the students,

2. the transparency of the process for examining the change, and

3. the word of those leading the change that it will proceed as promised.

All three pieces require effective communication of ideas, and current collaborative technologies can be of immense value for getting all involved to explore the possibilities and reasoning professionally.

VALUE OF THE CHANGE

When any member of the school team wants to propose a major change, a natural first step is to make the case. This is as much optimizing chances for success as it is modeling what good learning and (as we'll see) good writing is all about.

First, what is the change being proposed? Can it be brought down to a sentence or two?

Second, what is the issue or need the change attempts to address? This, too, should be summarized, and also backed with specific evidence as to why the change would be of value to students at the school. The use of data from well-conducted research (as opposed to careless research, which one can find in abundance in education) that aligns with a school's goals, technology plan, etc. likely will be an important component of this step.

Third, what are the anticipated concerns about the change? These should be written as favorably as possible so as to accurately represent the positions of those who might oppose the proposal. As soon as it looks like genuine concerns are being intentionally misrepresented, the exploration will move from professional discussion to political jockeying, and the potential will skyrocket for doing more harm than good to the team's sense of community.

Obviously, this third part regarding concerns should have effective counter-arguments to address the concerns. Ideally, teachers, whether they support or oppose the proposal, will all consider the process a fair, and even interesting, one that allows them to productively explore what they and their students need.

While the process described above may seem obvious for effectively communicating a proposal to a team, anyone who has worked in schools for at least a few years has probably seen multiple and mangled attempts to drive change without a clearly articulated proposal addressing needs and concerns.

TRANSPARENCY OF THE PROCESS

In addition to being able to describe with concise clarity the value of a proposal, keeping the process transparent is one area in which technology can be especially helpful. An online and collaborative document allows for developing the case, arguments, and counter-arguments in such a way that any member of the team can review the process and make suggestions for how to move forward with the exploration.

Imagine the change of schedule, for example. A document that everyone can easily find and comment on allows building discussions effectively. The drivers of the change may be the only ones with editing access to the main document, but multiple other documents can be linked to the main one, allowing members of the team to carefully articulate concerns and hopes for the change.

Allowing anyone on the team to write up questions and concerns that link to the main document does more than show that no one will be ignored. It also can raise the level of discussion by making it clear whose arguments are well-constructed.

Structurally, the main document might be organized something like this:

- title

- summary of the proposal

- detailed proposal with links to supporting documents

- lists of questions, concerns, and comments, including summaries of positions with names and links to other documents with detailed arguments

- timetable for next steps in process

- notes regarding major changes in proposal during process

The twin benefits of a truly open process are clear enough:

First, the proposal for change is best crafted by tapping the insights of the entire team, with the obvious goal of catching issues before they arise during implementation.

Second, articulated ideas with careful reasoning, along with adjustments made for credible concerns, keep the exploration from becoming a political drama in which people whisper that their objections were never taken seriously.

If your school also undergoes regular accreditation visits, keeping a process of exploring change organized in easily accessed online documents might serve as evidence for how you characterize your team's strengths, as well.

> *Proposals for change are best crafted by tapping the insights of the entire team.*

PROGRESSION AS PROMISED

Finally, there is in the exploration the opportunity to build trust that the school's leaders keep their word. Exploring major change offers this chance for building trust, and just as easily can result in destroying trust and the ability to work together effectively.

One way of looking at how change is implemented is to compare the proposal at the beginning with what emerges at the end. If there are no major differences between the two, it's possible one will come to the conclusion that consulting the staff was mere lip service, and consequently a waste of time. Following a process for documenting the consideration and implementation of a proposal in the previous section can do much to avoid such conclusions.

Using identified changes that were incorporated from team members' concerns and a careful elaboration of why other suggestions were rejected from the final plan, leaders can get to a point where the team's strengthened professionalism that came from the process proved at least as valuable as the change itself.

At Serra, the initial proposal for a block schedule was tried as a two-week pilot in the spring ahead of the anticipated adoption. The teachers were surveyed, and results showed that they didn't like the model.

The leadership postponed the adoption and worked with teachers to craft a better model, which was tried the following spring. This time, surveys were positive and the switch to a block schedule went forward successfully.

Had the leaders who proposed the change stuck to their original plan they would likely still be dealing with the pushback. By being willing to make adjustments and find their way to something that worked for everyone, they ended up with a successful change.

Technology is only a tool. Explorations of major change show that using strong, collaborative communication tools well can build trust and professionalism, and everyone benefits from that.

And as my friend Tammy Maginity of Pennfield Schools in Michigan would note, this also is modelling the effective use of collaborative tools. Once teachers are comfortable with techniques you use as part of your work with them, they are in a far better position to try them out with their students.

What changes are on the horizon for your school? How will you make exploring that change something that strengthens your entire team?

BUILDING A TEAM

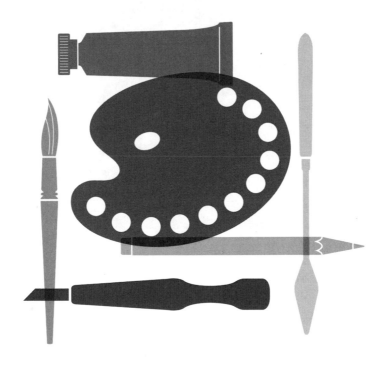

CHAPTER 10

Tech and Hiring Teachers, Part 1 - Those Who Can Take the Reins

Among the critical elements of building the best possible team, perhaps the most obvious is effective hiring, so when your leadership team meets to talk about what kind of people you hope to attract, it is best to get very honest with yourselves, very quickly.

Are you looking for people who will create dynamic learning opportunities for students? If so, those you hire might well already have an idea of what resources the school will need to make available to allow them to design these learning experiences. If the candidates don't bring it up themselves, it is a good idea to ask those you interview what they will need for what you hope they will contribute.

Are you looking for capable but compliant people? If you are looking to cultivate leaders from among your team, then compliant to the point of not asking questions may not represent much in the way of promise for future leaders.

For the long-term health of the school, one of a leader's most important roles is the development of talented people who may not yet understand their potential for leadership. Look for people who are capable of pushing back on ideas in a way that is constructive, as you will need for every member of the leadership team, including yourself, to be genuinely capable of working well with people who sometimes question a school's direction.

Most leaders would give lip service to that being important. Not all these leaders actually have the tact and patience to engage in discussion on why given decisions were made so as to build teamwork and confidence in their leadership, however.

> *One of a leader's most important roles is the development of talented people who may not yet understand their potential for leadership.*

Imagine two responses to a decision to purchase a site-wide license for a fictional online reading tool we'll call WondeRead:

Teacher A: "Is WondeRead the best choice for us?"

Teacher B: "I think you're making a mistake."

Both teachers are questioning the decision. Teacher A is tactful, though not clear about his or her opinion. Teacher B provides clarity, though may not be earning points for tact.

Let's assume that the leader isn't one who gets upset about merely having decisions questioned, and is perfectly aware that however well or poorly it may be worded, a teacher may have good reason to call the decision into question.

The leader might even see two opportunities: first, to get info to know whether to continue with the purchase of the license, and second, to help the teacher develop skills should that person move on to leadership at some point in the future.

Leader: "Well, we still have time to make a change. Can you provide me some details with evidence for doing something different?"

In an interview with a prospective teacher, you can ask a number of questions or prompts related to technology that give you a good idea how this person will communicate as part of future discussions:

- "Describe a time when you and a colleague disagreed about using technology as part of a lesson."

- "Tell me about your experience choosing a particular tech tool for an activity you did with your students. I'd be especially interested in one for which another tool was being considered."

- "How do you see technology in terms of telling the stories of the learning that happens in your classroom with the larger community?"

- "What has impressed you or raised a concern about how our school uses social media?"

Ideally, the prospective teachers will show themselves to be people who can describe what they know in a way that invites constructive discussion. The ever-changing nature of technology means we are always able to learn something new with any given tool or resource, so discussions about possibilities can arise at any time.

The easier it is for members of a team to talk constructively about what they both know and don't know, the easier it will be to make good decisions for everyone.

Looking ahead, these are the discussions that can set leadership coaching in motion, as well. My friend Aubrey Patterson, a former superintendent of the Lloydminster Catholic School Division in Saskatchewan, Canada, sees the path like this:

1. Tech is a natural avenue for identifying teachers who can act as coaches. Good use of tech is as much about good teaching and learning as it is about how to use any given tool.

2. Teachers who prove to be good tech coaches are the first in line when identifying good candidates for school administrators. Again, it isn't about the tech they know, but how they show they can communicate good ideas to colleagues.

3. School administrators who show that they can couple good communication about teaching and learning with strong organizational skills with leading teams are the first in line when identifying good candidates for district-level positions.

Tech's role, in short, is less about tech and more about what we do with what we have. Good leaders make the most of who and what is at hand.

How can you and your leadership team develop and use the humility to find and listen to those who question your decisions?

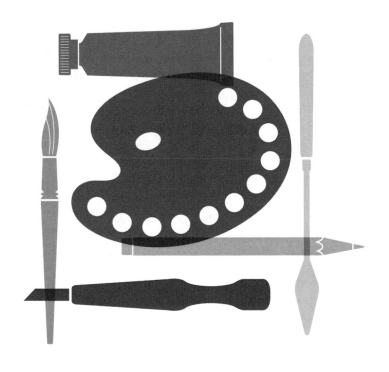

CHAPTER 11

Tech and Hiring Teachers, Part 2 - Teachers and Technology

Let's note two truths and zero in on teachers (though what's below could easily apply to administrators, as well):

1. There are strong teachers who know little to nothing about technology.

2. There are teachers who know plenty about technology but aren't very good at teaching.

One job of the person interviewing candidates is to figure out whether the prospective teacher falls into either category above. If the first, is the person open to learning new things? That may be less a question for the candidate and more for his or her references. If it turns out the person has a history of turning down opportunities to develop new skills, it is likely this isn't the kind of teacher who can contribute meaningfully to a school with a genuine exploratory culture.

If the candidate is in the second category, he or she probably isn't a good match for any school that has the ability to be choosy about whom to hire. The first order of business, clearly, is to have creative insights on how to help kids learn and an ability to implement interesting ideas.

Ideally, your prospective teacher should be able to do both of the below:

1. Use technology to extend learning in powerfully memorable ways that are impossible without technology, and

2. Be able to articulate why this is good for students' learning and growth to parents and other teachers.

Conversations that come from what a teacher can do with technology can go well beyond what that person brings to your school. These topics can give you a glimpse of the teacher's ability to create moments of cool on your campus.

- "Have your students ever taught you something about using technology for critical thinking and deeper learning?"

- "When your students do something that goes well, how do you share that with colleagues?"

- "Can you describe a moment when a student used any kind of tool or resource in your class, and blew away everyone with how interesting it was?"

- "What's a crazy idea you have tried with your teaching?"

Explanations for what prompted crazy ideas might allow you to see how interviewees might contribute to an exploratory culture. Whether they seek help from colleagues might give a hint about strengths related to teamwork. How they presented their ideas to team and campus leaders might give a sense of how organized they can be.

Regardless, you'll have something to bring up when talking with references in order to do the all-important job of getting past the quick answers and figure out what's genuinely interesting (or worrisome) about a candidate.

Good interviews also can allow you and your team to get ideas from new hires that generate strong conversations about what can populate an explore-for-the-future list. This is the kind of list you pull out on a regular basis to encourage creative brainstorming, and items from the list are also good prompts for tapping insights of teachers, staff, and parents in informal conversations.

In the last chapter I mentioned how Aubrey Patterson used tech as a vehicle for identifying leaders. In the realm of seeding good brainstorming, here is another space where his example is one worth considering widely.

Aubrey's leadership team would discuss interviews, book studies, etc., and was therefore well-positioned to identify items for what Aubrey calls the "BF file." "BF" stands for "bring forward," and so in addition to identifying good material for future conversations, someone would be identified as responsible for bringing the item back to the team on a given date.

These are clear expectations about being organized and perhaps even creative with sharing ideas about the item to be discussed. A leader who can come back in several months to an item mentioned once in a conversation is demonstrating both faith in the members of the team and a focus on tapping the team's talents for the benefit of the school.

There are many ways technology can be valuable in a school. If you are looking to hire the best teachers you can, discussions of tech's potential can optimize your chances of finding great matches for your students and the larger professional team. Knowing someone can use technology effectively for sharing stories of success is a major plus in considering any candidate, and may help you do what is needed to build support in your community for what happens at your school.

How do you learn from those you interview? How can you convey that you are someone who regularly learns new things, just as you expect that from your team?

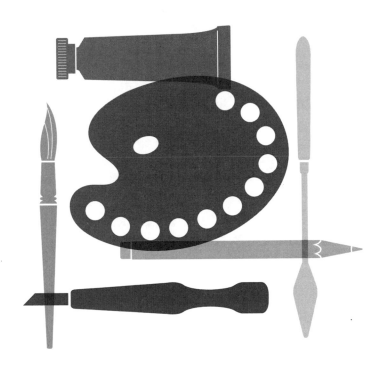

CHAPTER 12

Tech and Hiring Teachers, Part 3 - Going Deeper

"He was great in the interview."

All those who have worked hard to find good candidates for schools and businesses know very well the context for the sentence above.

The person we chose was easy to talk to, full of ideas, and could point to experiences such that we were confident she or he would be a wonderful addition to the team.

And soon after the person started, it became clear that what was covered in the interview somehow managed to miss (or mislead from) weaknesses as a team player, tendencies that work against the school's goals, inconsistencies in professionalism, etc.

While there is no fail-safe method for avoiding the bad actor who cleans up well for an interview, there are tools that can allow us to get a better idea of who we're dealing with than in the past.

Several years ago, I led a team that formed and launched the Rotary eClub of Silicon Valley. You are likely familiar with service clubs (Rotary, Lions, Kiwanis, Soroptimist, etc.), and mine is one with a couple of twists: it's online and it's asynchronous.

Our members are spread across multiple continents. Making sure prospective members have a heart for serving others and a track record that proves it is no small task.

How do we know that the person will be a good fit with our online group? Will this be someone who can contribute to who we are and what we do, rather than be a whiner who saps the energy of other volunteers? Is this someone with the self-discipline needed to contribute actively to our efforts? And, not unimportantly, is this person any fun?

One of our members is a man who learned about us and contacted us directly without any initial reference from another Rotarian (what we call ourselves in Rotary - there are 1.2 million Rotarians around the world working to improve communities near and far).

Learning about him, though, turned out to be fairly easy. The prospective member has a highly unusual name, and I was able to do a simple search in social media to see what I would find.

As it turns out, he has a massive digital footprint. In particular, his Instagram account shows that he has traveled all over the world, his comments in his posts going back years speak to a positive outlook, and his activities often focus on projects to help others.

Does that mean he would be a good fit? Not definitively, but like anything else, it's part of a larger picture.

Use a social media footprint to build a set of questions that explore what matters to the candidate. Seeding conversations is one way tech can help get you further along the path toward understanding someone's potential.

> **Use a candidate's social media footprint to build a set of questions that explore what matters to this person.**

Another useful tool is a recorded interview. While this could be a recording of a face-to-face meeting, let's explore what might be possible with a recorded video conference.

Let me note that the tools for recording a video conference/chat/call are now easy to learn and freely available. Zoom.us, for example, gives you the ability with its free tool to record conversations (with a time limitation when more than two people are connecting) and save the video online or onto your computer.

Many of the advantages of using video conferences may be obvious, such as not requiring a candidate who lives far away to have to travel to your school for the initial interview.

You also might learn something about candidates from their choices of where to connect to talk with you. Have they picked a place that is crowded and makes conversation difficult? If connecting from home, is there something about the room where he or she is that tells you something interesting, such as a poster or a trophy? Did the person still go to the trouble of dressing professionally, even though the meeting isn't in person?

It is always appropriate, of course, to ask the candidate if it is okay to record the conversation. Your main reasons are to be able to review the ideas the person shares, and to allow others on your team who aren't present at the meeting to watch the conversation later.

Keep in mind that how you come across is equally important to finding a good match, and the tips below can help you set the stage well for a good discussion:

- Position your face so that you are close enough to the screen to be seen and heard properly. Having an angle that puts you in the bottom half of the screen can make it difficult for the candidate to pick up on visual cues he or she would see in a face-to-face meeting.

- Position yourself so that the camera catches your face in the light, rather than the shadows. One of the worst ways to run afoul of this concern is to sit with the camera facing a window with light streaming in. Simply put, being interviewed by a silhouette is probably not going to give a good message to the candidate.

- Understand what kinds of ambient noise might interrupt the conversation. Are you doing this at a time when announcements will happen over a loudspeaker? Have you chosen a moment when people outside your office might be working loudly? Is there a fan near the computer that will distract either of you?

- Adjust if the connection is a poor one. It would be better to reschedule than to spend half the conversation trying to figure out what the last thing someone said was.

- Never forget that what you are saying in a recorded interview is for an audience larger than the candidate. How you come across in the recording can be for others on your team a lesson in tact, insight, or a complete lack of either.

Other members of the leadership team who review the conversation also might offer ideas for more questions in a follow-up interview, and the discussion with your leadership teammate could generate ideas that are valuable to the school.

The more members of your team who provide feedback on a candidate, the better the chances that you won't have someone weak slip through your processes for hiring.

What is a new way your team might work together to evaluate potential hires?

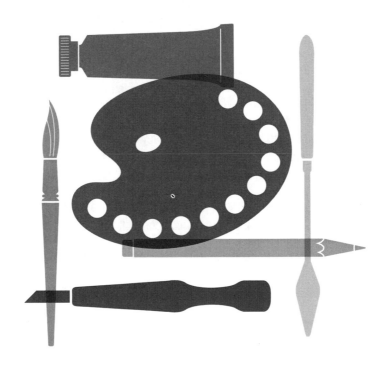

CHAPTER 13

Tech and Hiring Teachers, Part 4 - Interviewing and Being Interviewed

Understand that an interview works both ways.

Strong candidates want to know how interesting the school is, and whoever is conducting the interview is the face of the school. Candidates want to know if there is a culture of respect for teachers among leaders. They want to know if this will be a team they can be proud to be part of. They want to know how faith and academics intertwine at your school.

Before I took my first job as a principal, I set up several interviews for other positions. I was waiting on final board approval for the principal position, and wanted to explore backup avenues should something go wrong.

One of the large districts in the city had an opening for a Japanese language teaching position, and as I'd had a decade of building a successful program, I submitted an application. I love language teaching, and thoroughly enjoy helping American teens appreciate the very different approach to communication that characterizes Japanese.

The HR person who interviewed me, though, seemed fairly aloof. I didn't think much about her demeanor initially, as I know everyone has bad days. I figured my job was to see if I could get her excited about the kinds of things I've done before and could bring to students in her district.

At the end, she asked if I had any questions, so I asked several. I asked about support for the program, and what kinds of resources were available. I asked about processes for taking groups of students on overseas trips, which I'd enjoyed doing before. In short, I asked what I'd be able to do if I were one of their teachers.

Later, I learned in contacting the district that a decision had been made not to offer me the position. A bit of an ego bruise, that was, but perhaps there were plenty of good candidates and I simply hadn't made the cut. Given my previous experiences, I did find it a little odd that they hadn't called to say so, and I decided to contact a friend in the district to see what I could learn.

Much more interesting than my not being offered the position, though, was the comment from the HR person my friend passed along to me:

"It felt like we were the ones being interviewed."

My thinking is that if an interviewee is asking detailed questions about where he or she will work, that's a good sign. In this case, it apparently wasn't. It's also possible that something else I said or did let her know I wouldn't be a good match. The comment, though, was telling.

Do you believe absolutely anyone can teach the students at your school? If so, then you may not want people who will stand up and ask hard questions about how the school serves the students.

On the other hand, if you believe that finding the most talented people possible for your school is important for reaching every last student, then look for people who can navigate difficult topics tactfully and professionally - people you would be happy to represent your school in the community.

Every interview works two ways. Finding people who will ask good questions is not just a function of adding, "We are looking for a motivated, professional person for the position," to the job description. It also requires representing your school properly when you conduct an interview.

> *Look for people who can navigate difficult topics tactfully and professionally - people you would be happy to represent your school in the community.*

In the introduction for *The National Standards and Benchmarks for Effective Catholic Elementary and Secondary Schools* (NSBECES) it is noted that the mission of our schools is "to proclaim the Gospel, to build community, and to serve our brothers and sisters."

How you come across to interviewees is one clear way you convey what your school is about, and whether people from the outside will know if your school lives up to the three-fold mission described in the NSBECES.

What do you hope to convey to those who interview for positions at your school? How do you know whether you've succeeded?

FOSTERING
EXCELLENCE

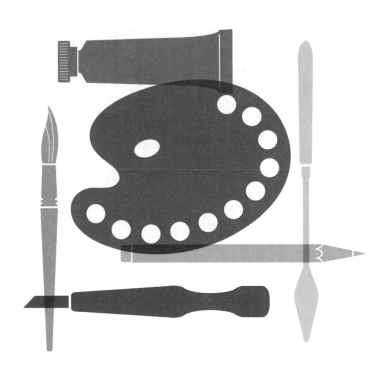

CHAPTER 14

Teacher Resilience and Documentation

A friend once described an experience with a colleague. In the colleague's first year, she had an unusually well-behaved class, and she finished the year full of confidence.

The pendulum swung mightily with her second year group, and as she looked at the roster ahead of the beginning of school, it was full of students with challenges she had heard about from others.

"How am I supposed to teach this group?" she asked my friend.

This is a moment, and it's worth exploring possible responses he might have given.

Imagine that a teacher in the same situation has asked this question. You, one of the instructional leaders on campus, have the benefit of that teacher's tone and facial expressions for gauging your own response, of course, but establishing some clarity is likely a strong first move, perhaps with something like the following:

"There are two ways I could take such a question.

"It may be that you feel you don't have the expertise for these kinds of challenges, and are reaching out for help on what to do because you want to be a teacher who has the skills such students need.

"It's also possible you're suggesting to me that you've already decided that your relationship with them will be one of conflict and failure.

"Help me know which way you were leaning when you asked the question, and I'll know how I can help."

It is obvious that how the person reacts to this will tell you plenty about his or her potential to grow as a teacher and a colleague.

It also is something you should note, literally.

Many administrators, being very busy, don't take time to make notes about conversations that can be critical in later evaluating a teacher's resilience when deciding whether to renew a teacher's contract, grant tenure, etc. A simple form that allows you to choose the teacher's name from a list and make a note could be of importance later.

Such a form is something you can create yourself using any note-taking tool, or perhaps the survey tool mentioned in several previous chapters (Google Forms), and the fields could be:

- name of staff member

- date

- time

- circumstances (the facts - no judgments)

- thoughts (your sense of why the encounter is important)

Using Google Forms means your entries feed a spreadsheet, and what goes in can be sorted easily. Using a multiple choice or drop-down for the names is a good move, too. If you have to pull all the notes for one teacher at some point, a simple misspelling or difference between nickname and formal name, for example, won't cause you to miss one of the entries.

Your documentation can be valuable as fodder for identifying additional coaching the teacher may need. It may serve as the reasons the teacher is to be let go. The key is that you are organized so as to help the teacher and the school.

Additionally, the more organized you are, the better your chances that an employee will choose to do the right thing at a difficult moment. That is to say that there are those who will choose a less honorable path when, due to the leader's lack of organization, they feel they can get away with it.

> *The more organized you are, the better your chances that an employee will choose to do the right thing at a difficult moment.*

Coming back to the teacher in the story that opened this chapter, your entry may reflect a crisis in confidence and foreshadow a problem-plagued year for the teacher and perhaps also for you, if you are the one supervising this person.

At the moment asked, you may get a more promising reply, and should the teacher choose to open up to learning something new, you'll want to note that, as well.

This also creates the opportunity to paint a larger picture as you help this teacher develop:

"This will certainly be a different group than the one you had last year. That said, we hired you because we see in you the potential to be someone who reaches kids that are tough cases - students others may have given up on. You'll need help, but we believe that in your care many of these students can learn to love who they are and can be."

Make sure, of course, you don't simply walk away from such a statement with this teacher struggling to swim in the deep end of the pool. Follow up with regular check-ins and connections to people who can help the teacher accomplish what you believe is possible.

Creating connections with others is another good thing to note in your form. Regularly reviewing the form's entries, and especially when you are preparing to visit the teacher, can keep you from missing something important that you might have said or done to help that teacher be successful.

The teacher we have discussed in the example would need to work hard in the months that follow to develop the resilient character great teachers have, and you would need to know that you didn't step away from your responsibility to be a meaningful resource.

How do you help teachers become more resilient? What can you do to be more organized with the advice you give?

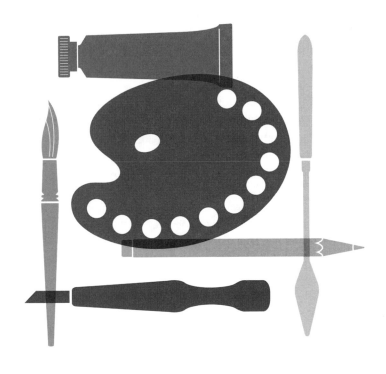

CHAPTER 15

Identifying and Expanding on Strengths

One underlying fear of many teachers is that a leader will ask them to make changes that sacrifice things they do well, and shift toward that with which they have little confidence.

While you can articulate your interest in preserving the strengths a team brings to a school, your actions will speak louder in addressing this underlying concern.

The chances are good that you are in a setting where some of the teachers have taught for many years, perhaps for decades. However long they have been at your school, it also is likely you have some who may have become jaded or lack enthusiasm for giving their all to exploring new possibilities. Still, almost all of them should be able to point to great moments of learning and teaching they have experienced since joining the team.

Take the opportunity of sitting down to ask people about great moments from the past. You may well learn about stories that should be captured and celebrated by the larger community. These members of the staff may know people (such as alumni or church connections) who are close by and would visit in order to inspire current students. You may discover a teacher's personal and professional interests which, if encouraged, may support fascinating learning activities.

Just as rapport with students is the basis for a great classroom, rapport with staff is the hallmark of a leader who is able to help a school grow in meaningful ways. This rapport a leader has with a team often determines how they feel they are supported when trying something new, and one easy way of testing this is with experimentation and discussion of new technology tools.

This gets us back to the topic of fear.

When a more traditional teacher of any age does something really well, making a change can be daunting - a concern that something that teacher loves and has confidence doing might go away. Assuming a given strength truly is something good for student learning, your focus could be to convey that this teacher's talent or activity can be expanded in an interesting way using some sort of technology.

As one would hope is clear to any teacher or educational leader, technology shouldn't be used simply to be able to say one is using technology. Rather, the idea is that any given tool can allow an amplification of possibilities or an uncovering of something new.

As an example, imagine a teacher who is particularly strong with feedback on writing. The teacher spends plenty of time marking up papers, having students work with each other on approaches to improving their work, and articulating how the word and structural choices matter for various audiences.

It may be that using collaborative writing tools allows more feedback from others in and beyond the classroom than they have had before. The teacher can require students to take feedback and evaluate it for use in their work before handing it in to the teacher. After all, it's certainly promising when a student can defend why she chose not to follow a particular piece of advice, or can build upon a good piece of advice he received and explain why it strengthened his writing.

That this feedback might be from a wider variety of sources than is available in the classroom is all the better, and is made more easily available with any number of communication technologies.

Using simple audio or video tools, this teacher might be able to create media with insights that students can listen to or watch when they are most ready to benefit from the teacher's ideas.

Using a simple screencasting tool, students might go on to create their own recordings, with the idea of building a library which can help current classmates and future students.

This teacher may begin to use amazing images from all over the world available via social media to serve as a limitless set of prompts for great writing and feedback opportunities.

You may find examples of great writing in blogs that you read. You might find pithy insights on Twitter or Pinterest. You might find interesting videos on Vimeo or YouTube. For our purposes, let's use an image and story from Instagram.

This post is from Karen Mandau, a travel photographer who shares thoughtful and compelling stories on that platform:

A strong writing teacher who hasn't used technology before would have little trouble getting students to begin exploring questions and connecting pieces of the image into a story, one for which they need to gather and evaluate feedback from others in and out of the class.

The teacher might also share the written addition to the picture in Mandau's post:

> *"Those who have seen my previous post already know this charming gentleman, Mr. Lung Toa.*

> *"When we brought him the prints of the photos we took of him he was very excited. He told us that this was the first time he has ever gotten his picture taken, and that he was very happy because now, when he will die, his children will be able to remember him.*

> *"To anybody who takes travel portraits, I strongly encourage you to get a travel printer and give the people you photograph a print. To some it will be nothing, but to many, like Lung Toa, this small gesture can be a precious gift."*[1]

The story opens up new possibilities for discussion and writing, and a teacher who learns how to find great images online can enrich the students' learning experience immeasurably, particularly if the next step is tapping into the ideas of others through get-togethers or online communities.

At the 2018 Illinois Computing in Education conference[2], I presented a session on dynamic prompts from online sources, and asked the teachers in the room to share ideas for the Mandau post, above. Here are some of their responses:

- How can you observe others around you in order to appreciate their culture and differences?

- What type of world (literally and figuratively) does this man live in that this would be the first time he's ever had a photo taken?

- What are five questions you would ask this man if you met him today?

- Does an increase of images/photos reduce their value because for this man, this one photo holds tremendous value?

- Are there other things this man could have never experienced that you have?

- How do you want to be remembered?

As we engaged in the activity, teachers could see in our chat stream what others were suggesting as prompts, and the longer they had to consider what others had done, the better their suggested questions.

Feedback is powerful. Using technology, we can increase the ways we gather and evaluate feedback. The teacher whose strength is feedback now has more tools in the belt for doing something he or she loves.

Little things we do clearly can have a big impact on others. The time you take to learn the details of strengths of the members of your team can make an impression that lasts well beyond the interaction.

Asking teachers for past strengths may both convey that you are not asking them to give up on things they know work, and also that working together, these activities may prove all the more valuable to current and future students.

Thinking about your conversations with members of your team, as with the last prompt above, how do you want to be remembered by those who have worked with you?

1 Karen Mandau's post on Instagram; used with permission (available at: https://www.instagram.com/p/BQOGf6olERR/)

2 Illinois Computing in Education (available at: https://www.iceberg.org/)

CHAPTER 16

Valuing the Stories of the Entire Team

Every adult who works on your campus is someone who can provide insights as to what your school and students need.

Valuing the stories of different people on a team can translate into reaching more students in powerful ways, and often, those stories come straight from the mouths of the most vulnerable students:

"For the first time I could sleep through the night..."

The woman I was speaking with was quoting a kindergartner. It seems that student had come to her house to spend the night with her child, who was a good friend.

As she told me this, she caught herself, clearly becoming emotional. She took a deep breath, and gave it another shot.

"For the first time I could sleep through the night, because it smelled clean."

Her eyes were filling with tears. The moment had happened more than twenty years before, but the power of a child's simple statement was still moving to her.

It is one thing to be reminded that some of the children we serve would find a clean room and bed to be something out of the ordinary.

It is another to know that the parent telling the story is an employee of the district I was visiting. But she is not a teacher.

We often extol the role of teachers in the lives of children, and rightly so, but it seems rare that we properly recognize that there is a whole team of people working to help children see their potential.

There are bus drivers who greet children in the morning, and they may well be the first smile a child encounters each day. These are people who see the neighborhoods and the homes, as well as the interactions a child has with parents, siblings, and other children. They may be the first to see the behavior of a child showing signs of becoming a bully.

There are custodians who see students in the halls and on the playground. They see hurts and kindnesses that others don't. They see in a red-inked, crumpled page in the trash the frustrations of students who want to learn but are becoming convinced they are incapable.

There are servers in the cafeteria who learn quickly, through simple observation, which children can't count on a meal after they leave school. They know which students are grateful to have something given freely.

There are secretaries who see students arrive at school each day, and know from facial expressions which ones are already battling the demons of worry and friendlessness.

> *We often extol the role of teachers in the lives of children, and rightly so, but it seems rare that we properly recognize that there is a whole team of people working to help children see their potential.*

All of these people and many others have perspectives on the children that teachers and administrators may not.

In valuing stories, know that it is not just a matter of listening; you can help the members of your team have experiences that become the stories that improve their lives and your school.

Franklin Community Schools, the Indiana district where I met the person who told me the story earlier, is a place where any member of the team can apply for a grant to help them become better at what they do. In working with them, I have been given time with numerous teams of support staff. I have seen how the district's leadership values everyone, and how that helps students.

As a school leader, you do or do not tap into these stories that guide you toward possibilities for helping children in need.

You do or do not give these members of your team avenues for communicating with you via a phone call, text, and/or online form.

You do or do not convey to all members of the team that they are partners in the job of figuring out how to reach the next kid.

Finding ways to foster and share the stories of the members of the team who do not teach, though, may do much more than help your teachers appreciate these colleagues. Powerful stories, like the one about the kindergartner above, are those that can move us from being mired in day-to-day frustrations back to keeping kids' needs and challenges at the forefront of our thoughts and conversations.

Every focused and productive member of a school team is working to create an atmosphere that optimizes the chances for inspiring kids, and you likely have more power to accelerate that than anyone else on your campus.

How does the team know whether you value the contributions of everyone?

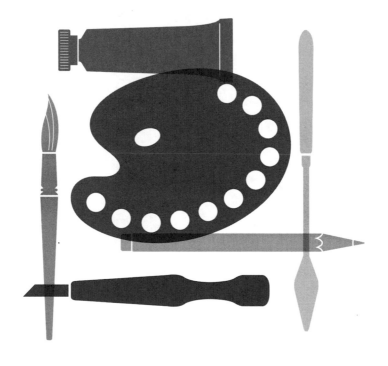

CHAPTER 17

The Aspirin Teacher and the Log of Good Moments

Anyone who has worked with a school staff has known someone I gently refer to as, "The Aspirin Teacher."

This is the teacher who comes into your presence, looks at you, and your head starts to ache.

This person's comments are double-edged exemplars of one with an established history of excellence in the realm of the passive-aggressive.

This person has developed Olympic-level skill at turning a normal conversation on improvement into a swamp of concerns that reflect problems across the campus and in society at large.

The kids and/or colleagues are always at fault.

The verbal aikido that allows The Aspirin Teacher to redirect any attempt to discuss possibilities for improvement toward anything else mirrors the skills of the least honorable politicians.

All of that to say, when talking with this person, it may prove challenging to draw upon the kind of compassion taught by Jesus.

And despite all this talent for bringing throbbing pain to your temples, this teacher wants to do well, too.

All teachers want to finish the day feeling they have inspired students. All teachers want to feel they are respected and effective at what they do. Remembering this may be the entry point for making something constructive happen.

There are several reasons this teacher's conversations with leaders and colleagues have become more about conflict than cooperation.

Understand that people walk into any conversation with thoughts about all sorts of personal and professional concerns, some of which have to do with the job at hand. Many relate to events completely beyond the leader's control. Reminding yourself that you don't know the full picture can keep you from engaging in a conflict that is serving to distract the teacher from the real pain he or she feels.

> ## *All teachers want to finish the day feeling they have inspired students.*

One thing a leader might ask every teacher to do is to keep a log of good moments that remind them why they teach. What gets added to the log can be a small victory in class getting a student past something challenging, a laugh that comes from a clever comment a child shares, or perhaps a connection to the community that brings an inspiring speaker or fascinating resources to the classroom.

It can be anything. The key is that it's something positive.

A teacher who engages in conflict with you or colleagues regularly is someone who needs to have a positive reference point. Requiring that each member of one's team keep a log of good moments creates an avenue for buying needed time to move from frustration or anger to constructive conversation.

At one school where I work, I am regularly struck by the vulnerability and celebration that come from sharing what is on each person's heart when a staff meeting opens with prayer requests. A log of good moments can allow for many more opportunities for thanksgiving with colleagues.

It can be an articulated expectation that when the leader asks what recently has been added to the log of good moments, any member of the team is able to set aside momentary frustration to speak of what they've logged. The understood promise is that you and that member of the team will return to the concern, but your assessment is that a brief departure from that conversation could be constructive in dealing with the concern more effectively.

And in the spirit of always knowing both the carrots and the sticks that are in play, it should be considered a serious issue if the adult is unable to switch conversations out of a lack of self-control regarding whatever he or she is angry about.

Many of these moments can remain private, but when it comes time for a member of the team to move to another school, having a log of good moments you can both easily access. You both may want to discuss which moments over time best represent that person's contributions as you prepare a reference.

Employees should get regular opportunities to pause and add to their good moments log. Not only is it an easy way to make the atmosphere a little more positive, it might also act like an aspirin for those moments when one's head is hurting.

How do leaders you admire help team members get past their frustrations? What might you try at your school?

CHAPTER 18

Psychology and Excellence

Great leadership involves the ability to set in motion that which makes members of your team understand they are capable of achieving more than they imagine.

You can't do this without encountering barriers.

The forces working against individual and group improvement are numerous, and one of the simplest is an unconscious reverence of convenience. Columbia Law Professor Tim Wu (most famous for coining the term "net neutrality") captures this issue well in his essay "The Tyranny of Convenience"[1]:

> *"The dream of convenience is premised on the nightmare of physical work. But is physical work always a nightmare? Do we really want to be emancipated from all of it? Perhaps our humanity is sometimes expressed in inconvenient actions and time-consuming pursuits. Perhaps this is why, with every advance of convenience, there have always been those who resist it. They resist out of stubbornness, yes (and because they have the luxury to do so), but also because they see a threat to their sense of who they are, to their feeling of control over things that matter to them."*

There is obviously a tie between technology and convenience. Much of the tech we buy is supposed to simplify work processes, after all.

However, let's also note that "this will make [insert work process here] easier" is never a marketing tagline for games. Gaming holds a special fascination for so many of our students, who spend untold hours working their way through the challenges embedded in games of all descriptions.

> *Set in motion that which makes members of your team understand they are capable of achieving more than they imagine.*

So let's engage in a thought experiment:

1. School leaders want their students to accomplish great things.

2. Great things typically require hard work.

3. Many students think of hard work as, at best, a necessary evil.

4. These same students may play games that require immense amounts of effort and concentration.

The disconnect between the third and fourth items represents an opportunity.

As a high school teacher many years ago, I remember watching students who had trouble pushing themselves to turn in short homework assignments. These same students would spend hours after school in my classroom in order to create movies for the projects they knew we would all watch together.

In other words, there was plenty of evidence that my students were willing to work hard, as long as they meaningfully connected with what they were doing. Admittedly, that didn't describe every homework assignment I asked them to do.

In many schools I have seen this heightened effort from students in a variety of settings, from athletics to service efforts to intriguing class projects that are presented to larger audiences.

The effort breaks down quickly, though, when the outcome is seen as a mere hoop to jump through in order to satisfy what seems to them an arbitrary requirement.

At this point, we can note that while we have been using students for the thought experiment, there is little difference between their efforts and how many of the adults on your campus see what they are required to do by you or other leaders in the hierarchy.

If teachers are asked to provide lesson plans in a format you've specified, for example, do they feel that these plans are part of a larger process that makes what they do better and more interesting for their students and themselves?

If not, then the requirement needs to lead to something different and interesting, or abandoned as something that runs the real risk of making people cynical rather than being that which encourages them to foster and share excellence in their classrooms.

In Nampa, Idaho, there is an elementary school I have visited to work with their teams, and every Tuesday morning there is an optional gathering called "Coffee & Convo." Someone brings coffee, someone brings doughnuts, and they engage in a little convo, or conversation. Typically, a quarter to a third of the staff will attend these optional meetings. They talk about great moments that have happened over the last week, and together they celebrate students' successes.

The psychology here doesn't require a doctorate to understand.

The leaders, Tami Vandeventer and Alanna Parsons, have set up an environment in which people comfortably talk about successes and celebrate the accomplishments of students and colleagues.

The teachers and other staff members watch for and work toward that which will be the basis of another success to share. And when the entire team gets together in other meetings, this very positive group sets the tone.

In other words, they are willing to put forth the effort needed to make things happen for kids. It's a teacher version of the previously mentioned disconnect, overcome.

Let's revisit the last line in the quote from Tim Wu's New York Times post:

> *"They resist out of stubbornness, yes (and because they have the luxury to do so), but also because they see a threat to their sense of who they are, to their feeling of control over things that matter to them."*

For our Coffee & Convo crowd, they don't see others' successes as a threat to their sense of who they are, and are comfortable being experimental with things that matter to them.

Without doubt, the work of the leaders (Vandeventer, the principal, and Parsons, the lead instructional coach) has set the stage for the teachers and non-teaching team members to think more constructively about their capabilities. They sidestepped convenience, and the result is a team that is now proud of their school and themselves.

Even more satisfying than winning a game, that is.

What are ways you have seen teachers and support staff engage each other to go above and beyond their work requirements?

1 "The Tyranny of Convenience" by Tim Wu; NYTimes.com, posted Feb 16, 2018, and accessed Aug 26, 2018 (available at: https://www.nytimes.com/2018/02/16/opinion/sunday/tyranny-convenience.html)

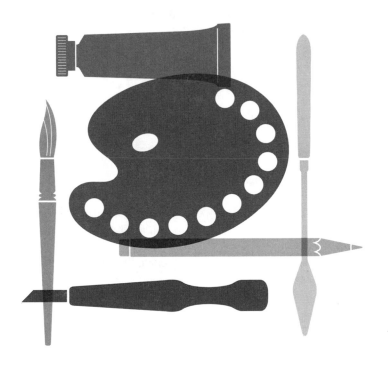

CHAPTER 19

Excellence and the Leadership Team

For some schools, having a team made up of the principal or head of school, deans or associate principals, grade level representatives, and department leaders allows for meaningful exploration of the team's perspectives and goals. The different members of the team know that they can share what they are thinking and seeing, and others around campus know that the team will take seriously their concerns.

For some schools, that is.

For others, this leadership team is present, but it serves to channel frustration, complaints, and downright whining in such a way as to leave all concerned depressed about the chances for together building something more personally and professionally uplifting.

When the atmosphere of a leadership team is negative, there are two things to know:

1. It can improve.

2. It will take doing something different than what is being done now.

Those may seem forehead-slappingly obvious, but plenty of schools have leaders who despair without trying to trod different paths with their teams, even when the evidence is clear that something different needs to happen.

That may be because we are quick to go with what we know, even when what we know isn't effective, or even pleasant. That clearly isn't limited to leadership; weak educators excel in repetition of the unsuccessful.

Success in new things is a function not primarily of what is tried, but of establishing that the team is one which can comfortably experiment.

Experimentation also can be limited in its point of departure. Leaders who require themselves to be the ones that generate the ideas moving things in a better direction may actually be generating the very barrier that keeps needed ideas from coming forward. The best atmosphere for sharing ideas is one that comes from trust that all players on the team will honor each other's thoughts and look for the possibilities even in those ideas that at first seem unhelpful.

> ## *Weak educators excel in repetition of the unsuccessful.*

Creating this atmosphere with a leadership team is no small task, but the first step may be to articulate expectations with a topic for which there is no dispute on the need.

"Alright, we know that we have a bullying problem. We've tried messages in the announcements and posters on campus, and it hasn't helped.

"I'm looking for new ideas, and they can be downright crazy. The key is that the idea gives us something to try, and that we agree on how and when we'll measure whether it helps.

"As a reminder, you are all on this team because you are capable of contributing what is needed to make this school better for everyone. That includes my expectation that the ideas we come up with here stay here until we are ready to share them with others.

"That is to say, your honor, insights, and willingness to value each other are why you're here and why I think we can come up with something better than we have so far."

Note that value of the term, "crazy."

When asked for good ideas, some people won't contribute a thought because they feel it doesn't rise to the standard expected. When a group is willing to entertain crazy ideas, then almost anything can be explored.

The final part of the message regarding why people are on the leadership team may sound more explicit than is needed at your school, but it is highly unlikely that such a message would do any harm. Professional excellence is a function of both word and deed, and no one is in a better position than the leader to create an atmosphere that fosters it.

Excellence on the leadership team certainly makes a school stronger, though it is worth adding that if a leader is doing a superb job of building that team, then people will likely be leaving it from time to time to share their leadership experiences with other schools.

This is all to say that it is important to build a culture of trust and exploration on the leadership team, and it is equally important to find those on the larger staff who will be able to take on more responsibility when positions become open.

One approach to building the local talent pool is to manufacture more leadership opportunities. Give your teachers the chance to head up initiatives with the community, and be prepared to talk regularly with them to help them develop their out-of-classroom skills.

This could be as simple as asking one of your teachers to connect with people from the diocese and report about professional development opportunities that will come available in the next year or two. Let your diocesan colleagues know you'll be asking someone to contact them; they'll likely be happy to help you develop your teachers who show promise for leadership.

You also can ask your teachers about contacts they have in the community who might be able to support the school in some fashion - guest speakers, project sponsors, etc. Not only might this generate good moments for the school, but it gives you another avenue of professional discussion with members of your staff, and therefore another way of assessing who might be the best candidates when positions open.

I have been in environments in which the leader was so capable that others simply waited on that person to do things. Excellence on the team, though, comes from knowing both when to let someone else take the reins, and how to encourage them to do things they might not have done before.

How might your leadership team make itself stronger?

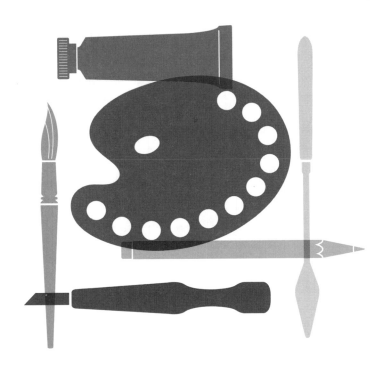

CHAPTER 20

Modeling Reliability

How do we teach students how to make good decisions?

A teacher who says one thing and does another is at best losing the opportunity to teach something important, and at worst teaching that words, not deeds, are what matter in the classroom. When a bad model has been established, any student caught not living up to an honor code can point to the hypocritical example as a defense.

School leaders are in a similar position with the staff. A staff member caught not living up to professional expectations might well point to the example of a leader who, like the teacher mentioned here, says one thing and does another.

There are any number of ways poor leadership exemplifies this. For our purposes, let's choose one of the simplest ways a leader can fail a member of the team: not following through on a promise.

> **When a bad model has been established, anyone caught not living up to an honor code can point to the hypocritical example as a defense.**

If you encounter a teacher on campus and that person asks you to do something, how do you make sure you will get it done?

Clearly it can be hard when trying to handle several things at once to remember all that you discuss. That said, if you know you have committed to something, however small, are you able to act on it and let the teacher know the outcome? That is to ask, does your team know you will always follow through on your word?

There are any number of ways leaders work to do this. Some carry a notebook and check things off as they get them handled. A perfectly good system, if (a) the leader doesn't lose the notebook, and (b) he or she has it available when needed.

Others use one of any number of task list apps. Having something on a mobile device is clearly useful, assuming the app gets used regularly.

I'll describe a way that works for me. What is important for you is that whatever system you use to avoid letting people down works consistently. Knowing what will work well starts with knowing what motivates you.

There are many things that motivate me. My wife's happiness is at the top of list. Finding fun and possibilities in systems and how to make systems effective also is important, though perhaps not as common in the larger population as the one at the top of my set.

I'll focus on something less noble, but still well up my list: my email inbox.

I love, love, love moving things out of the inbox and having the number of remaining notes be something I can take in at a glance. On incredibly rare occasions, I've reached zero, and each time it has happened, I'm quite sure there were clouds parting and angels singing.

The online calendar I use has a feature that can be set as a default, and this feature is where I do well in terms of organization. As the time approaches for an event, the system generates an email reminder. The email appears in my inbox, where, knowing my outlook on the world, you know I really want to get it handled.

A day in my calendar may include several items set before 6:00 a.m. That's almost never because I've scheduled something then. Rather, it's because having an item in the calendar then will mean that when I first check my email in the morning, I'll see the generated reminders. Handling them provides the added pleasure of removing items from the inbox.

And the people said, "Amen."

This may qualify me as easily entertained, but it also means I do a pretty good job of handling what needs doing. If I don't get something done, it may well be because I tried building the reminder in some other way that didn't play to my quirk about the inbox.

Turn your quirks into working systems, and let those systems help your people know that they can rely on you.

What you model has an effect on the decisions of your team, just as what teachers model has an effect on the choices of students.

What is one of your quirks? Can you use it to become more reliable?

THE
FINISH

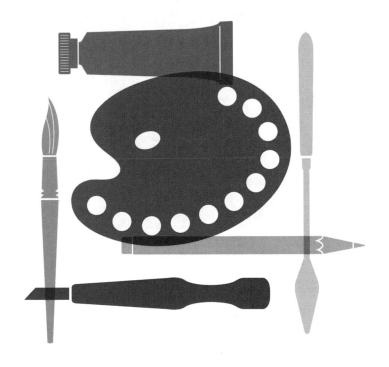

CHAPTER 21

Fostering Loyalty

I have been a service club person for a long time. Connecting with others who have a heart for making a difference for people in need is something I find energizing.

Several years ago, I spoke at a Kiwanis club in San Jose, California. Several members of the club are graduates of Catholic high schools, and while I don't know their exact ages, Al, the man I have in mind has, I suspect, the triple digits in sight.

The day I was there included "Happy/Sad Dollars," which as an activity is a staple of this particular club. The idea is that for a few minutes, the basket gets passed around, and anyone who wants to do so can toss a few dollars in the basket and share a celebratory item, complain about something, etc.

Al energetically tossed in some bills, and expressed his enthusiasm over the result of a football game of St. Ignatius, the college prep school in San Francisco he attended sometime in the far distant past. He then launched solo into a school chant-song-thing that generated all sorts of good-natured eye-rolling around the room.

But what generates an Al? What creates the connection that means that many decades from now, people continue to pay attention to what happens at the school, and might even break into song, given the chance?

I believe my high school had a song, as I have a dim memory of it being on a wall somewhere. I can never recall our singing it together, and am not sure I've given the topic any thought since the early 1980s. Were the fate of the world relying on my singing the song, we would all be doomed.

This is not to say I had a bad high school experience; on the contrary, I have many good memories from that time. What I don't have is the kind of ingrained connection that Al does with St. Ignatius.

What I do have now, though, is a wealth of experiences with a variety of schools all over the world, and will finish this book focusing on three elements I've learned that I think are critical for fostering loyalty from staff, students, and their families.

INSPIRING EXPERIENCES

Students at truly exceptional schools have experiences that allow them to see themselves from new perspectives.

They connect with people, ideas, and possibilities both on campus and far beyond it, giving them confidence that they can contribute in their immediate setting and understand something of the larger world around them.

Today, that includes using tools that allow them to interact with others in faraway places, creatively craft connections among things learned across subjects, and ask critical questions about, and pursue answers for, what they encounter in any setting.

Done well, their experiences inspire them to accomplish something new, and to understand themselves as people capable of doing much more than jumping through hoops.

In his book published by NCEA, *Charism and Culture: Cultivating Catholic Identity In Catholic Schools*, Dr Timothy Cook speaks of a school's distinctiveness in terms of what it wants from its graduates[1]. He draws a difference between highlighting what is provided students, and who students become as a result of their experiences at the school.

Every graduate of your school is a testament to what you and your team work to achieve. Students' personal successes obviously should start well before they leave, and every adult plays a part in inspiring students to push themselves and recognize that their effort leads to successes that their families at home and at the school can celebrate.

DEDICATED PROFESSIONALS

It is not enough to have talented and organized individuals leading classes and running all aspects of the school. For students and their families to connect on a personal level with the school, they must see that the adults function as a team in some distinctive fashion.

No matter one's job at a school, doing it well creates the conditions that allow children to be inspired, and this in turn creates powerful professional connections. Working together, the school's professionals generate experiences as a symphony generates music, as opposed to the discordant sounds of even talented individuals playing separate songs all at the same time.

These professionals also create the kind of welcoming environment that make the school a place where students feel safe to think, to explore, to question, and to be. Beautiful architecture and grounds can certainly serve this purpose, but without the effort and exploration of talented, caring professionals to create personal and educational connections that build confidence and hope, learning does not lead to the highest levels of inspired, school-connected success.

> *Working together, the school's professionals generate experiences as a symphony generates music, as opposed to the discordant sounds of even talented individuals playing separate songs all at the same time.*

REGULAR STORYTELLING

Successes must be shared. In the best schools, students and adults alike are comfortable with, and regularly engage in, sharing moments that can lead to shaping new successes.

This is most powerful when the students themselves have had the chance to craft their experiences. Doing well on a test is one thing; creating something that inspires the community to see new possibilities is at a much higher level.

Successes that become shared stories allow for moments of identification with the group. Families talk to each other about great moments of learning, such as when students from their school that did well in a robotics contest, or advocated for an accessible playground in the community, or created a video about their connection to students in another country.

Connections with alumni also generate not simply moments of pride, but new stories from the opportunities these alumni have to connect as mentors or classroom guests. These stories of their participation can create the enthusiasm needed for alumni to work together to support new initiatives of the school, thereby generating more stories of inspiring successes.

A school that does all of this well leaves lifelong impressions on the students.

Perhaps many decades from now, proof of that will come as one of your students breaks into song.

What I hope I have accomplished in this chapter and this book is to convey the interplay within a culture of exploration that prepares the ground for the best kind of educational and professional experiences.

Schools are places of service, and that focus in a Catholic setting is what draws many of those who become the most dedicated and supportive families. Others may come for the strong academics and impressive alumni community, but soon realize that exploration of faith and demonstration of service are at least as valuable in helping children become adults who find joy and meaning in their lives.

I hope the ideas in this book inspire you to see possibilities in your school you haven't seen before. Many of these ideas begin with what technology makes possible, but like the best experiences, they end with what happens in people's hearts.

Thank you for taking time to read what I have written. You can find me at my blog at rushtonh.com, and I hope you will reach out to me to share ideas on ways I can improve the messages I give, in the hopes that will help others to see new possibilities, as well.

Finally, may you regularly inspire your students and each other, and may your stories generate successes on and well beyond your campuses for many years to come.

1 Charism and Culture: Cultivating Catholic Identity In Catholic Schools, by Dr Timothy Cook (pp 59-60) (available at: https://www.amazon.com/Charism-Culture-Cultivating-Catholic-Identity-ebook/dp/B00YHMQXQ2)